THE
GILDED
AGE

edited by
Ari Hoogenboom and
Olive Hoogenboom

Prentice-Hall, Inc. *Englewood Cliffs, New Jersey*

A SPECTRUM BOOK

*For Irwin, Al, Jerry, Fred, Charlotte, Joel, Bob B., Bob M.,
Joe, Paul G., Paul H., Kaye, Mike, Sara Lee, Pete, Ibby,
Sid, Harold H., Harold M., Marcy, Frank, David A.,
David D., David S., Jaki, John K., John M., Caroline,
Dick, Steve, Allan, Lou, Marv, Jim, Ernie, Mr. Munro, and
the rest of the crew at the Library of Congress.*

ARI HOOGENBOOM is Professor of American History at
The Pennsylvania State University, and has taught at
many universities, including the University of Texas
(El Paso) and Columbia University. He was a
Guggenheim Fellow during 1965-66, and is
past Secretary of the Pennsylvania Historical Association.

OLIVE HOOGENBOOM has worked as her husband's
research assistant since 1955. She is currently
collaborating with him on several other projects.

Current printing (last number):
10 9 8 7 6 5 4 3 2 1

CONTENTS

INTRODUCTION, 1

I
RAILROADS

III
THE FARM

IV
LABOR

V
IMMIGRATION

VI
THE CITY

VII
EDUCATION

VIII
POLITICS

The Politicians

Civil Service Reform

The Tariff

Currency

Imperialism

INTRODUCTION

The Gilded Age is only one of many epithets that describe the era from 1865 to 1900. Book and course titles tell us that it was an age of excess, that it was an age of America's transition into modern times, of industry's coming of age, of the decline of *laissez faire* and individualism, of the search for order and nationalization of daily life.

Between 1865 and 1900 great technological innovations in communication and production both required and made possible the organization, consolidation, and nationalization of American society. Revolutionary techniques of extracting and transporting raw materials, of fabricating and distributing finished products, of transporting people to and from work, of providing for multitudes in huge cities, and of collecting and disseminating information changed American life. Durng these years a few large-scale operators gained control of most of the significant industry, laborers and farmers organized while cities and their problems multiplied. The federal bureaucracy was transformed and ideas of classic liberalism—*laissez faire* and individualism—were undermined by experimental pragmatism and positive governmental action.

The following eyewitness accounts cover many of these developments and evoke the spirit of the age—a spirit that is both antique and modern. By rattling on a train across New Jersey with Mark Twain, attending college with Julia Foraker, or dropping in on Ole Man Pickett's place in Cincinnati, we are thrust into a bygone era. Yet many of the eyewitness accounts are strikingly relevant to our own times. The Gilded Age grappled with problems still with us today—problems created by big machines, big business, big labor, big farmers, big cities, and big government—problems that were taking shape during this dynamic era.

The machine-made problems of monopoly and automation; the urban problems of slums, transportation, sanitation, and crime; the rural problems of material and cultural poverty; the failure to educate adequately the children of immigrant and Negro minorities; and the world-wide commitment of the United States rooted and matured during the Gilded Age. What could be more current than William James's psychedelic experiment with *mescal,* the contrast between planter John C. Calhoun's views of the Negro and those of Negro editor T. Thomas Fortune, or Theodore Roosevelt's attack upon the academic community for daring to advocate peace? We are constantly struck by how remote the Gilded Age is in some respects yet in other ways how close it seems; by how long we have traveled yet how short is the distance that separates us.

I

RAILROADS

The Gilded Age could concentrate its energies only as rapidly as communications would permit. A communications revolution enabled industrialists to exploit distant sources of raw materials and to profit from nation-wide markets; cities to multiply in number and size; farmers to push into remote regions, expand their holdings, and specialize their production for distant cities; and society to move rapidly from local and regional to national standards of manners and morals, values and goals, tastes and styles, ideas and information. Important though the telegraph and telephone were, the great transformer of American society was the railroad. Growing from 35,000 miles of track in 1865 to 193,000 miles in 1900, soaking up billions of invested dollars, railroads posed an insoluable problem as well as an inestimable blessing for the Gilded Age. How was society, stubbornly adhering to economic individualism and *laissez faire,* to cope with powerful economic agglomerations that made competition a mockery but achieved efficiencies society did not wish to sacrifice? Something had to give, and in the end it was *laissez faire.*

[1.]   *"The Generation . . .
        Was Already Mortgaged to the Railroads"*

Returning from Europe with his family, Henry Adams finds American society dominated by the "great mechanical energies." [Henry Adams, *The Education of Henry Adams: An Autobiography* (Boston: Houghton Mifflin Company, 1918), pp. 237-40. Reprinted by permission of Houghton Mifflin Company and Constable & Co. Ltd.]

How much its [i.e., American society's] character had changed or was changing, they could not wholly know, and they could but partly feel. For that matter, the land itself knew no more than they. Society in America was always trying, almost as blindly as an earthworm, to realize and understand itself; to catch up with its own head, and to twist about in search of its tail. Society offered the profile of a long, straggling caravan, stretching loosely towards the prairies, its few score of leaders far in advance and its millions of immigrants, negroes, and Indians far in the rear, somewhere in archaic time. It enjoyed the vast advantage over Europe that all seemed, for the moment, to move in one direction, while Europe wasted most of its energy in trying several contradictory movements at once; but whenever Europe or Asia should be polarized or oriented towards the same point, America might easily lose her lead. Meanwhile each newcomer needed to slip into a place as near the head of the caravan as possible, and needed most to know where the leaders could be found.

One could divine pretty nearly where the force lay, since the last ten years had given to the great mechanical energies—coal, iron, steam—a distinct superiority in power over the old industrial elements—agriculture, handwork, and learning; but the result of this revolution on a survivor from the fifties resembled the action of the earthworm; he twisted about, in vain, to recover his starting-point; he could no longer see his own trail; he had become an estray; a flotsam or jetsam of wreckage; a belated reveller, or a scholar-gipsy like Matthew Arnold's. His world was dead. . . .

One comfort he could enjoy to the full. Little as he might be fitted for the work that was before him, he had only to look at his father and [the historian John Lothrop] Motley to see figures less fitted for it than he. All were equally survivals from the forties—bric-à-brac from the time of Louis Philippe; stylists; doctrinaires; ornaments that had been more or less suited to the colonial architecture, but which never had much value in Desbrosses Street or Fifth Avenue. They could scarcely have earned five dollars a day in any modern industry. The men who commanded high pay were as a rule not ornamental. Even Commodore Vanderbilt and Jay Gould lacked social charm. Doubtless the country needed ornament—needed it very badly indeed—but it needed energy still more, and capital most of all, for its supply was ridiculously out of proportion to its wants. On the new scale of power, merely to make the continent habitable for civilized people would require an immediate outlay that would have bankrupted the world. As yet, no portion of the world except a few narrow stretches of western Europe had ever been tolerably provided

with the essentials of comfort and convenience; to fit out an entire continent with roads and the decencies of life would exhaust the credit of
the entire planet. . . . From the moment that railways were introduced,
life took on extravagance.

Thus the belated reveller who landed in the dark at the Desbrosses
Street ferry, found his energies exhausted in the effort to see his own
length. The new Americans, of whom he was to be one, must, whether
they were fit or unfit, create a world of their own, a science, a society, a
philosophy, a universe, where they had not yet created a road or even
learned to dig their own iron. They had no time for thought; they saw,
and could see, nothing beyond their day's work; their attitude to the
universe outside them was that of the deep-sea fish. Above all, they naturally and intensely disliked to be told what to do, and how to do it, by
men who took their ideas and their methods from the abstract theories
of history, philosophy, or theology. They knew enough to know that their
world was one of energies quite new.

. . . Society knew as much as this, and seemed rather inclined to
boast of it, at least on the stump; but the leaders of industry betrayed no
sentiment, popular or other. They used, without qualm, whatever instru-
ments they found at hand. They had been obliged, in 1861, to turn aside
and waste immense energy in settling what had been settled a thousand
years before, and should never have been revived. At prodigious expense,
by sheer force, they broke resistance down, leaving everything but the
mere fact of power untouched, since nothing else had a solution. Race
and thought were beyond reach. Having cleared its path so far, society
went back to its work, and threw itself on that which stood first—its
roads. The field was vast; altogether beyond its power to control offhand;
and society dropped every thought of dealing with anything more than the
single fraction called a railway system. This relatively small part of its
task was still so big as to need the energies of a generation, for it required
all the new machinery to be created—capital, banks, mines, furnaces, shops,
power-houses, technical knowledge, mechanical population, together with
a steady remodelling of social and political habits, ideas, and institutions
to fit the new scale and suit the new conditions. The generation between
1865 and 1895 was already mortgaged to the railways, and no one knew
it better than the generation itself.

[2.]   *"How We Built the Union Pacific"*

Chief Engineer of the Union Pacific Railroad Grenville M.
Dodge captures the spirit of the enterprise. [Grenville M.
Dodge, *How We Built the Union Pacific Railway* . . . , Senate Document No. 447, 61st Cong., 2d sess., 1910 (Washington, D. C.: United States Government Printing Office, 1910),
pp. 13-15, 31, 15, 24-5.]

The organization for work on the plains away from civilization was
as follows: Each of our surveying parties consisted of a chief, who was
an experienced engineer, two assistants, also civil engineers, rodmen,
flagmen, and chainmen, generally graduated civil engineers but without
personal experience in the field, besides axmen, teamsters, and herders.
When the party was expected to live upon the game of the country a
hunter was added. Each party would thus consist of from eighteen to
twenty-two men, all armed. When operating in a hostile Indian country
they were regularly drilled, though after the civil war this was unnecessary, as most of them had been in the army. Each party entering a
country occupied by hostile Indians was generally furnished with a military
escort of from ten men to a company under a competent officer. The duty
of this escort was to protect the party when in camp. In the field the
escort usually occupied prominent hills commanding the territory in which
the work was to be done, so as to head off sudden attacks by the Indians. Notwithstanding this protection, the parties were often attacked,
their chief or some of their men killed or wounded, and their stock run off.

In preliminary surveys in the open country a party would run from 8
to 12 miles of line in a day. On location in an open country 3 or 4 miles
would be covered, but in a mountainous country generally not to exceed
a mile. All hands worked from daylight to dark, the country being recon-
noitered ahead of them by the chief, who indicated the streams to follow,
and the controlling points in summits and river crossings. The party of
location that followed the preliminary surveys had the maps and profiles
of the line selected for location and devoted its energies to obtaining a
line of the lowest grades and the least curvature that the country would
admit.

The location party in our work on the Union Pacific was followed by
the construction corps, grading generally 100 miles at a time. That distance

was graded in about thirty days on the plains, as a rule, but in the mountains we sometimes had to open our grading several hundred miles ahead of our track in order to complete the grading by the time the track should reach it. All the supplies for this work had to be hauled from the end of the track, and the wagon transportation was enormous. At one time we were using at least 10,000 animals, and most of the time from 8,000 to 10,000 laborers. The bridge gangs always worked from 5 to 20 miles ahead of the track, and it was seldom that the track waited for a bridge. To supply 1 mile of track with material and supplies required about 40 cars, as on the plains everything, rails, ties, bridging, fastenings, all railway supplies, fuel for locomotives and trains, and supplies for men and animals on the entire work, had to be transported from the Missouri River. Therefore, as we moved westward, every hundred miles added vastly to our transportation. Yet the work was so systematically planned and executed that I do not remember an instance in all the construction of the line of the work being delayed a single week for want of material. Each winter we planned the work for the next season. By the opening of spring, about April 1, every part of the machinery was in working order, and in no year did we fail to accomplish our work. . . .

• • •

It was not until after November, 1867, when we had been at work two years, that we got railroad communication with the East at Council Bluffs, Iowa, the initial point of the Union Pacific Railway, by the completion of the Northwestern Railway. Till then the Missouri River had been the sole route over which supplies could be had. It was available only about three months of the year, and our construction was limited by the quantities of rail and equipment that could be brought to us by boat in that time. In twelve months of work after we had rail communication, we located, built, and equipped 587 miles of road, working only from one end, transporting everything connected with it an average distance of 800 miles west of the Missouri River. This feat has not yet been surpassed. In accomplishing it we crossed the divide of the continent and two ranges of mountains, one of which was the Wasatch, where in the winter of 1868-69 we had to blast the earth the same as the rocks.

• • •

The track laying on the Union Pacific was a science. Mr. W. A. Bell, in an article on the Pacific Railroads, describes, after witnessing it, as follows:

We pundits of the far East, stood upon that embankment, only about a thousand miles this side of sunset, and backed westward before that hurrying corps of sturdy operators with a mingled feeling of amusement, curiosity, and profound respect. On they came. A light car, drawn by a single horse, gallops up to the front with its load of rails. Two men seize the end of a rail and start forward, the rest of the gang taking hold by twos, until it is clear of the car. They come forward at a run. At the word of command the rail is dropped in its place, right side up with care, while the same process goes on at the other side of the car. Less than thirty seconds to a rail for each gang, and so four rails go down to the minute. Quick work, you say, but the fellows on the Union Pacific are tremendously in earnest. The moment the car is empty it is tipped over on the side of the track to let the next loaded car pass it, and then it is tipped back again; and it is a sight to see it go flying back for another load, propelled by a horse at full gallop at the end of 60 or 80 feet of rope, ridden by a young Jehu, who drives furiously. Close behind the first gang come the gaugers, spikers, and bolters, and a lively time they make of it. It is a grand 'anvil chorus' that those sturdy sledges are playing across the plains. It is in a triple time, three strokes to the spike. There are 10 spikes to a rail, 400 rails to a mile, 1,800 miles to San Francisco—21,000,000 times are those sledges to be swung; 21,000,000 times are they to come down with their sharp punctuation before the great work of modern America is complete.

•   •   •

Our Indian troubles commenced in 1864 and lasted until the tracks joined at Promontory. We lost most of our men and stock while building from Fort Kearney to Bitter Creek. At that time every mile of road had to be surveyed, graded, tied, and bridged under military protection. The order to every surveying corps, grading, bridging, and tie outfit was never to run when attacked. All were required to be armed, and I do not know that the order was disobeyed in a single instance, nor did I ever hear that the Indians had driven a party permanently from its work. . . .

From the beginning to the completion of the road our success depended in a great measure on the cordial and active support of the army, especially its commander in chief, General Grant, and the commander of the Military Division of the West, General Sherman. . . .

•   •   •

The Central Pacific had made wonderful progress coming east, and we abandoned the work from Promontory to Humboldt Wells, bending all our efforts to meet them at Promontory. Between Ogden and Promontory each company graded a line, running side by side, and in some places one line was right above the other. The laborers upon the Central Pacific were Chinamen, while ours were Irishmen, and there was much ill-feeling between them. Our Irishmen were in the habit of firing their blasts in the cuts without giving warning to the Chinamen on the Central Pacific working right above them. From this cause several Chinamen were severely hurt. Complaint was made to me by the Central Pacific people, and I endeavored to have the contractors bring all hostilities to a close, but, for some reason or other, they failed to do so. One day the Chinamen, appreciating the situation, put in what is called a "grave" on their work, and when the Irishmen right under them were all at work let go their blast and buried several of our men. This brought about a truce at once. From that time the Irish laborers showed due respect for the Chinamen, and there was no further trouble.

When the two roads approached in May, 1869, we agreed to connect at the summit of Promontory Point, and the day was fixed so that trains could reach us from New York and California. We laid the rails to the junction point a day or two before the final closing. . . . The two trains pulled up facing each other, each crowded with workmen who sought advantageous positions to witness the ceremonies, and literally covered the cars. The officers and invited guests formed on each side of the track, leaving it open to the south. The telegraph lines had been brought to that point, so that in the final spiking as each blow was struck the telegraph recorded it at each connected office from the Atlantic to the Pacific. Prayer was offered, a number of spikes were driven in the two adjoining rails, each one of the prominent persons present taking a hand, but very few hitting the spikes, to the great amusement of the crowd. When the last spike was placed, light taps were given upon it by several officials, and it was finally driven home by the chief engineer of the Union Pacific Railway [i.e., the author]. The engineers ran up their locomotives until they touched, the engineer upon each engine breaking a bottle of champagne upon the other one, and thus the two roads were wedded into one great trunk line from the Atlantic to the Pacific. Spikes of silver and gold were brought specially for the occasion, and later were manufactured into miniature spikes as mementos of the occasion. It was a bright but cold day. After a few speeches we all took refuge in the Central Pacific cars, where wine flowed freely, and many speeches were made.

[3.] *How They Built the Union Pacific*

Congressman Jeremiah M. Wilson's Committee damns the men who financed and constructed the Union Pacific and questions them about their practices. [Select Committee on the Credit Mobilier, *Affairs of the Union Pacific Railroad Company,* House Report No. 78, 42d Cong., 3d sess., 1873 (Washington, D. C.: United States Government Printing Office, 1873), pp. iii, iv, 58-61, 241, 467-69, 471-72.]

This act [creating the Union Pacific] was not passed to further the personal interests of the corporators, nor for the advancement of commercial interests, nor for the convenience of the general public alone; but in addition to these the interests, present and future, of the Government, as such, were to be subserved. A great highway was to be created, the use of which for postal, military, and other purposes was to be secured to the Government "at all times," but particularly in time of war. . . . To make such a highway . . . required a strong solvent corporation, and when Congress . . . aided the enterprise with subsidies of lands and bonds, the corporators . . . were, . . . under the highest moral, to say nothing of legal or equitable obligations, to use the utmost degree of good faith toward the Government. . . .

Congress relied for the performance of these great trusts by the corporators upon their sense of public duty; upon the fact that they were to deal with and protect a large capital of their own which they were to pay in in money; upon the presence of five directors appointed by the President especially to represent the public interests, who were to own no stock; one of whom should be a member of every committee, standing or special; upon commissioners to be appointed by the President, who should examine and report upon the work as it progressed; in certain cases upon the certificate of the chief engineer, to be made upon his professional honor; and lastly, upon the reserved power to add to, alter, amend, or repeal the act.

Your committee find themselves constrained to report that the moneys borrowed by the corporation, under a power given them, only to meet the necessities of the construction and endowment of the road, have been distributed in dividends among the corporators; that the stock was issued, not to men who paid for it at par in money, but who paid for it at not more than 30 cents on the dollar in road making; that of the Government directors some of them have neglected their duties and others have been interested in the transactions by which the provisions of the organic law have been evaded; that at least one of the commissioners appointed by the President has been directly bribed to betray his trust by the gift of $25,000; that the chief engineer of the road [Grenville M. Dodge] was largely interested in the contracts for its construction; and that there has been an attempt to prevent the exercise of the reserved power in Congress by inducing influential members of Congress to become interested in the profits of the transaction. So that of the safeguards above enumerated none seems to be left but the sense of public duty of the corporators.

•   •   •

Testimony of Cornelius S. Bushnell,
member of the Union Pacific Railroad Company Board of Directors

Question. Do you know anything in relation to any distribution of the stock of the Credit Mobilier [the company constructing the Union Pacific] among members of Congress by Mr. Oakes Ames or any other person?—*Answer.* I do not. I know that I signed a paper, or vote, authorizing Mr. Oakes Ames to deliver some three hundred and odd or two hundred and odd shares of Credit Mobilier stock which he said he had disposed of in the spring of 1867, when I was disposing of that two or three hundred thousand dollars' worth that I have testified of.

Question. Did he tell you at that time to whom he had disposed of that stock?—*Answer.* He stated that he had sold it—part of it at least—to different gentlemen, members of Congress, and that they held him to his agreement, which was made when I was selling it at 95 and 97. He said . . . that as a matter of honor and right he thought he ought to be authorized to fulfill his agreement with them. . . .

· · ·

Question. Why did he confine the distribution to members of Congress? —*Answer.* He was in Washington at that time, (the spring of 1867,) a member of Congress himself, and his department of placing the stock was more naturally with his friends here, while I placed it in New York and New Haven. Congress adjourned, I think, in March—early in the spring of 1867 at all events, and it was not until the fall, or late in the year, that the parties, as I understood, came to him and held him to his promise. In the meantime, owing to the sale of those $10,000,000 in bonds that I spoke of, and our getting over the Black Hills, the stock had gone up to 160 and above; but because it had gone up I didn't feel that it was right for us to refuse to authorize Mr. Ames to carry out his contract of sale; I thought the parties were justly entitled to the stock, as much as those were who had bought of me.

Question. Did you ever hear Mr. Ames say that he wanted to place the stock where it would do most good?—*Answer.* No, sir; I heard him say that he thought it would be bad policy, and perhaps injurious to us, to break his agreement with those gentlemen here, members of Congress and others, and I concurred with him fully. . . .

· · ·

Question. Were you informed that those contracts which were made by Mr. Ames, those sales of stock to members of Congress, were accompanied by a guarantee that the persons receiving the stock should realize at least

10 per cent. on it?—*Answer*. I don't think a word of that was said. I never heard of it until I heard of it in the testimony.

• • •

Question. Was there any reason given why cash was not paid into the treasury for the sales of stock made?—*Answer*. I did not understand that the sales were concluded. He had only promised the stock to those parties at the last end of the session, and then he took this stock in fulfillment of his promise.

Question. If it was simply a promise and there was no bargain and sale, then why was there any obligation to let the stock go at the rate at which it was at the time the promise was made, when it was now so much higher?—*Answer*. I won't say that there was no sale. He had offered the stock and the parties had agreed to take it, but before he had got the certificates and delivered them Congress rose and these parties went home, and he did not meet them again until Congress came together the next winter.

• • •

Question. Were there sales made to anybody else than members of Congress on such terms as to be binding sales, and yet without the payment of money; and, if so, who was that somebody else?—*Answer*. There has no such sale been concluded that I know of, and the transfer made.

Question. No inquiries were made by your company how it happened that the sales made by Mr. Ames never had brought any cash into the treasury? . . .

. . . *Answer*. No; nothing occurred to me about it then.

Question. But you did consider that although there was no binding sale made in those cases, it was your honorary and legal obligation to let that stock go at par, it being then worth nearly double as much?—*Answer*. Yes; I have always lived up to my contracts, make or lose.

Question. What perplexes me is to understand how there was any contract there, when you say there was only a promise, but no sale.—*Answer*. Well, if he had offered them the stock and they had agreed to take it; but he could not get the stock before they had gone.

Question. That would be a sale.—*Answer*. Well, that is as I understood it; a sale.

Question. But a sale on credit?—*Answer*. Yes; for a short time.

• • •

Testimony of Peter A. Dey,
Chief Engineer until January 1865

Question. How much of the line had been located when you left the road?
—*Answer.* I think about two hundred miles.

Question. And that was the two hundred miles west of Omaha?—
Answer. Yes.

Question. Had there been estimates made on that portion of the line before you left the road?—*Answer.* Yes.

· · ·

Question. Were these estimates what you regarded as being fair estimates as to the cost of construction?—*Answer.* They were estimates in dollars and cents. My idea was that our estimates were large.

Question. Can you tell whether they went up as high as $50,000 a mile?
—*Answer.* I made an estimate of the road for the first one hundred miles from Omaha, which did run up to about that. I made another estimate, which was a good deal below that.

Question. Which was the correct estimate?—*Answer.* The lower one.

Question. How did you happen to make the estimate at $50,000 per mile?—*Answer.* Mr. John E. Henry, who was a kind of superintendent of construction, came on from New York with orders to make a large estimate.

· · ·

Question. From your knowledge of that portion of the line lying between Omaha and the one hundredth meridian, what could that portion of the road have been reasonably constructed for, taking into consideration the price of materials, the cost of transportation, &c.?—*Answer.* I should think that about $30,000 a mile would cover it, including equipments. This I give you from my recollection.

Question. If I understand you, you made an estimate which you returned to the office of the Union Pacific Railroad Company?—*Answer.* Yes.

Question. And afterward Mr. Henry came on, and under his instructions you made a second estimate?—*Answer.* Yes.

Question. And it was the second estimate that was up to about $50,000 a mile?—*Answer.* Yes. That was for a single track, with all the necessary equipments, sidings, stations, buildings, water-tanks, &c.

· · ·

Testimony of Webster Snyder,
General Superintendent of the Union Pacific Railroad
from May 1867 to July 1869

Question. Did you pay anything except mileage to any of . . . [the Government Commissioners] ?—*Answer.* I never paid anything except for mileage and services (whatever they were entitled to) but to one.

Question. Who was that one?—*Answer.* That one is dead.

Question. What was his name?—*Answer.* Cornelius Wendell.

Question. How much did you pay him?—*Answer.* Twenty-five thousand dollars.

Question. For what purpose or on what account did you pay him that $25,000?—*Answer.* He was appointed Government commissioner, and declined to act.

Question. In what respect did he decline to act?—*Answer.* He declined to take any action as Government commissioner.

•   •   •

Question. State to the committee what interview or interviews, conversation or conversations you had with Mr. Wendell on this subject?—*Answer.* Mr. Wendell was there several days, and looked over the road, but did not appear to pay much attention to it, or to anything else connected with the road.

Question. What did you do?—*Answer.* I did not do much; I talked with him when I met him.

Question. What did you say to him in that connection?—*Answer.* That I should like him to take action or to do something. We had applied at that time for the acceptance, I think, of eighty miles of the road, and the other commissioners were there ready to act. I said that the company had spent its money in good faith, and that he was delaying us and keeping the company out of millions of money, which I thought was unjust and unfair.

Question. Did you make any proposition to him with relation to this matter in order to induce him to act?—*Answer.* I did not.

Question. Did he make any proposition to you?—*Answer.* He did.

Question. What was that proposition?—*Answer.* To pay him $25,000.

•   •   •

Question. By what authority did you make this payment to Mr. Wendell?—*Answer.* On my own responsibility.

Question. Did you have any other authority but your own for doing it?—*Answer.* No, sir.

Question. Name all the persons with whom you conversed about the same before you made the payment?—*Answer.* I do not think I conversed with any body except Dr. [Thomas C.] Durant [vice-president and general manager].

•   •   •

Question. What did Dr. Durant say?—*Answer.* Dr. Durant said he would not authorize it.

•   •   •

Question. How could you reconcile it to yourself as an officer of that company to hand over that large amount of money to a person who had no right to make the claim. How did you justify yourself to your superiors when it was objected to by the vice-president?—*Answer.* It was absolutely necessary that something should be done.

Question. And you considered yourself the judge of that?—*Answer.* Yes, sir.

•   •   •

Question. You were acting on your individual responsibility?—*Answer.* I was acting on my responsibility as an officer of the road.

Question. But without reference to the instructions of the company?—*Answer.* The president and directors were in Boston and New York, and I was 800 or 900 miles west of the Missouri River.

Question. And you considered this simply as blackmailing?—*Answer.* Precisely; nothing more or less.

[4.]   *They Locked the Stove*
        "To Keep the Passengers
        from Burning Too Much Coal"

Mark Twain, who (along with Charles Dudley Warner) gave the Gilded Age its name, captures its flavor as he recounts two train rides. [Mark Twain, *Mark Twain's Travels with Mr. Brown . . . ,* ed. Franklin Walker and G. Ezra Dane (New York: Alfred A Knopf, 1940), pp. 122-24, 154-55.]

We took passage in the cars of the New Jersey Central at 8 P.M. of the 3d of March [1867], and left port in the midst of a cheerful snow-storm. I call it cheerful because there *is* something exquisitely satisfactory in whistling along through a shrouded land, following blindly wherever the demon in the lead may take you, yet sensible that he knows the way, and will steer his unerring course as faithfully as if it were noonday; sensible also that you are as safe there as anywhere, sitting with back against the bulkhead, and feet crossed on the next seat, and hat drawn down to shade the eyes from the lamp overhead—sitting thus by the comfortable fire, smoking placidly and dreaming of other times and other scenes, taking small heed of the storm without, yet scarcely conscious that it is snowing and is blowing drearily across the bleak moor as well, and that some people are out there suffering in it, and distressed, but that you ain't; that, on the contrary, you are perfectly happy, and tranquil, and satisfied, sitting thus, and smoking, and dreaming, and being timed and soothed by the clatter of the wheels—well, you know there *is* something unspeakably comfortable about it.

That was the way I felt from eight till a little after twelve; (the sleeping-cars were full and I had to sit up all night.) I had been talking latterly to a young soldier who had been all through the wars, from Bull Run to Lee's surrender—a beardless veteran full of battle experiences and tales of camp and prison life—and was now within a hundred miles of his home, almost, for the first time in six years—handsome, modest, honest, good-hearted boy of twenty-three, and more ready to tell about his school-boy days than his six charges at Antietam—but gone the warrior was, and I was alone. Then I began to feel crampy a little, and then chilly—and presently I noticed that the fire was very low, and remembered that I had seen no one doctor it for over three hours. I got up and tried to open the stove door, but could not do it. A drowsy neighbor said it was locked, to keep the passengers from burning too much coal! I looked again, and found the keyhole—so it was true. The man said this was done "on all them d——d Jersey monopoler roads." I grew chilly fast, then, and gradually grew peevish and fretful, also. I observed that the furniture was mean and old, and that the train moved slowly, and stopped to land a passenger every three hundred yards. After that, every time we stopped I cursed the railroad till we started again, and that afforded me some little satisfaction. I observed, also, that the usual mean man was aboard, who kept his window a little open to distress his fellows. And after that I noticed how fearfully dismal and unhappy the passengers looked, doubled up in uncomfortable attitudes on short seats in the dim, funereal light—like so many corpses, they looked, of people who had died of care and weariness. And then I said I would rather walk than travel that route again, and I wished the Company would burst up so completely that there wouldn't be money enough left to give the Directors Christian burial, but I hoped they might need it shortly.

I shall never be able to express how glad I was when the gray dawn stole over the plain, and the sun followed and cheered the scene, and the train stopped and I gave my limbs a grateful stretch, and steeped my sorrowful soul in inspiring coffee.

. . .

We came East in an express train this time. It had fewer inconvenient features about it than that gravel train we went West in. It had one important one, though. We never could get a complete meal. We could eat a few minutes at a time, very often, but there was not a great deal of satisfaction about that. About the time you get fairly to eating, they yell, "All aboard for Cleveland!" and you have to start. Brown said he ate eleven dollars' worth the first day and then got into the sleeping car hungry.

And there were the peddlers. I bought out the pop-corn boy to get rid of him, because I was trying to compose a poem for a young lady's album. But he came right back with a stock of peanuts. I took a few and hurried him away and he returned with some ice-cream candy. I do not like ice-cream candy and peanuts together, but I invested at once because a lucky rhyme had been born to me and I wanted to set it down before it slipped me. Then the scoundrel came back with tobacco and cigars, and afterwards with oranges, imitation ivory baby-whistles, fig-paste and apples, and then he went away and was gone some time, and I was encouraged to hope the train had run over him. Such was not the case. He was only keeping his most malignant outrage for the last. He was getting his literature ready. And from that time onward that degraded youth did nothing but march from one car to the other and afflict the passengers with specimen copies of the vilest blood and thunder romances on earth—"Lionel Warburton, or the Perjurer's Doom;" "Godfrey de Langley, or the Carnival of Blood;" "One-Eyed Bill, or the Desperado's Revenge"—those were some of his mildest works; and on their backs were pictures of stabbing affrays, and duels, and people shoving other people down precipices, and wretched wood cuts of women being rescued from terrific perils of all possible kinds—and they were always women who were so disgracefully homely that any right-minded man would take a placid satisfaction in seeing them suffer a sudden and a violent death. But that peddler peddled those books right along for hours together, and I gave up my poem and devoted all my energies to driving him away and trying to say things that would make him unhappy.

[5.]   "*The Railway Is the Real Government*"

A New York merchant attacks railroad power. [Simon
Sterne, *The Railway in Its Relation to Public and Private
Interests: Address of Simon Sterne before the Merchants
and Business Men of New-York at Steinway Hall, April 19,
1878* (New York: Press of the Chamber of Commerce, 1878),
pp. 14-15.]

That the settlement of this country would have been impossible at the
rate at which it has been settled; that the development of its wealth could
not have taken place at the rate at which that wealth has developed; that
our community could not have sprung from a few sparsely populated
States into a nation bearing equal rank with the foremost peoples of
the earth within the short period of forty years, if it had not been for the
railway, are incontestible truths. Therefore we felt grateful to the power
that made us great, and it became king.

It is my purpose to show you how the king has made himself ty-
rant. . . .

The railway exercises political power, firstly, by reason of its being a
great employer—as a matter of *esprit de corps* the employees will follow
the unconcealed inclination of the employer towards one or the other of
the political parties or nominees; secondly, by the expenditure of money
in elections. Mr. Gould stated before a Legislative Committee in 1874,
that he "was a democrat in democratic districts; republican in republican
districts; in a doubtful district he was doubtful; but in every district and
at all times he was an Erie man." In the same examination he admitted
that he sent money freely into the numerous districts of the State to influence nominations and elections for Senators and members of the As-
sembly. He cynically observed that he thought those investments better
than to wait until the men got to Albany. That the railway interest of our
State suggests, and not unfrequently dictates, appointments on Legislative
Railway Committees, has for twenty years been an open secret. Do you
think that it is an accident which puts Mr. WAGNER, the drawing-room
car manufacturer, at the head of the Senate Railway Committee of this
State? It is said that this is done to prevent the railways from being
blackmailed by threats of unfriendly legislation. But such a power will not
be used simply for the purposes of defence, and is frequently used to secure

friendly legislation. At all events, the railway alone should not be permitted to determine what is or is not the kind of legislation that it wants. As the most important single interest of the State which retains lawyers, and it generally has those of the highest ability, it cannot but exercise an influence upon an elective judiciary. Such an influence is not necessarily corrupt, but it will always make an ambitious man beware of unnecessarily offending so formidable an interest. As to the press, the railway is among the largest of advertisers, and it is an interest, therefore, not to be criticised with impunity; and perhaps finding that the press is not wholly under the influence of its advertising columns, railway kings have become large proprietors of stock in newspapers—investments which are supposed not to be made in the expectation of large dividends on such stock, nor for philanthropical and educational purposes. The wire-pulling politicians are, of course, more or less under the influence of a power that can give or withhold many votes and much money.

Hence the railway is the real government—two removes behind a fluctuating, temporal government, as represented by our State and National officers. It has all the substantial elements of power, without the responsibility connected with office. When any thing of real moment is to be done in the way of legislation in this State, and this condition of affairs is typical probably of all the other States, the great railway company's position on the question becomes frequently one of importance, and we are strongly reminded of the letter of the small boy in one of Tom Hood's effusions, who asks his friend to visit his home, and shows a profound knowledge of the influences at work in that friend's family in the terms, "Ask your sister to ask your father to ask your mother to let you come."

[6.] *"Circumstances . . . Often Justify . . . Apparent Discrimination"*

Edward Porter Alexander, Vice-President of the Louisville & Nashville Railroad, discusses railroad practices. [Edward Porter Alexander, *Reply to Questions of the Special Committee on Railroad Transportation of the New York Chamber of Commerce* (Louisville: Bradley, Gilbert & Mallory, 1881), pp. 7-10.]

Discrimination, so-called, of course, exists. It exists in every branch of trade and commerce in the world. . . .

But the railroads do not make the discriminations or differences themselves, and it is out of their power to entirely remove them. The Creator instituted them when He determined not to make his creation a dead level of mud and water, and all other material elements stirred up together in uniform solution, inhabited, perhaps, by a single variety of queer fish which would enjoy that sort of premises. And when He gathered the waters together, and raised up the dry land, and gave every large city— according to His own free will and pleasure—either some kind of a harbor or navigable river, and sometimes both, and left the little towns, in the interior, without any, then He laid the foundation of every so-called discrimination in freight rates which exists in the United States to-day. *Every one of them is simply a railroad trying to compete with a water-route.* On the water the Creator gives free right-of way, and maintains the road-bed and furnishes the motive power, if man is not too much hurried to wait on sailing vessels.

•   •   •

These discriminations, against communities, as above stated, are but the remnants of far greater discriminations, which existed before ever railroads were built. With the development and improvement of the railroad system, they have decreased year by year, and will continue to decrease; and, whenever railroad transportation can be so perfected, in all its branches, as to be rendered at an average price as low as water transportation, then they will disappear entirely. . . . So far as any discriminations exist simply against individuals, under like circumstances, I condemn them utterly; and I am sure no railroad manager can attempt to justify them. But circumstances, I think, will often justify cases of apparent discrimination which would be pronounced unjust where the circumstances are not understood.

. . . A single case of this sort will illustrate the whole subject, and can be discussed and referred to far more understandingly than abstract theories.

A certain Southern road runs through a country which produces a great deal of turpentine, and has made rates for the distilleries upon its line which are satisfactory, on the whole, to all its customers.

One of those customers is located near a river, beyond which there is a considerable virgin forest of pine. But the difficulty and expense of crossing the river, and its wide swamps, made it impossible for the distiller to bring the products of that forest to his distillery without a loss. He, therefore, represented the facts to the manager of the railroad, and proposed that if the railroad would reduce its rates upon the turpentine, which he would get *beyond* the river, enough to pay the expense of bringing it over, he would build a ferry and a causeway through the swamp, and bring into cultivation the forest which was inaccessible, at the ordinary rates of freight.

The arrangement was made, and proved satisfactory and profitable to both parties. The turpentine distiller continued to pay, cheerfully, the original rates upon all products of the forest on his side of the river. For the turpentine he brought across the river at a considerable expense, he paid a lower rate of freight, which left him the same profit as on his original productions. The railroad company got the steady hauling of the products of this forest, which would have otherwise gone to waste and benefited no one. The owner of the forest received a royalty on his trees, bringing him an income which he could never otherwise have derived. A number of laborers received daily employment which they could not otherwise have gotten. And the whole mercantile community which is interested in naval stores received the benefit of the increased production.

Who was injured?

Nobody that I have ever heard of. Yet, if there had been any law against discrimination, that railroad manager could not have made that concession in rates to the distiller, without, at the same time, reducing his rates for hauling turpentine to every other distillery upon the road.

[7.] *"The Shadow Has Been Substituted for the Substance"*

T. V. Powderly, Grand Master Workman of the Knights of Labor, pronounces the Interstate Commerce Commission a failure and calls for a nationalized railway system. [T. V. Powderly, "Government Ownership of Railways," *The Arena*, VII, No. 1 (December 1892), 58-60.]

Every reasoning being is satisfied that if no private corporation should construct a line of railroad, where necessity arose, it would be the duty of government to supply the demand. It is an established fact that the government has not only the right and power to construct lines of transportation, but that it is the duty of the state to place such agencies at the disposal of the people when public convenience requires it. That the government has no doubt of its right to exercise a supervision of the railroads, is demonstrated in the existence of the Interstate Commerce Commission, which attempts to exercise a control over the railroads of the nation. In the early part of 1886 the Senate of the United States took up the question of railroad extortions, discriminations, etc., and appointed a committee to take testimony. The report of that committee occupies some fifteen hundred pages, and in summing up they allege that the complaints against the railroads are based on eighteen charges, which they present to Congress. The one offence which stands out clearly in nearly all of the charges is "unjust discrimination." "Reckless combinations," "watered, dishonest stock," "breaches of faith," and many other offences are charged. As a result of that report Congress enacted a law which went into effect in April, 1887, and the Interstate Commerce Commission has been a public institution ever since. During the debates on that bill the railroad lobby was energetic and active. The intent of the framer of the bill was that the law should give control of the railroads to the commission, to be appointed; but the combined railroad interests of the country secured the emasculation of the bill, and it received the signature of the president in such a form as to be almost worthless except to provide places for a few individuals. That commission has been at work for five years; and with the exception of the arrest and punishment, by fine, of one freight agent, no punishment has been meted out to offenders against public welfare. Unjust discrimination still continues, reckless combinations are entered into with less attempt at concealment than before; passes are issued to legislators, judges, county officials, governors, and clergymen in greater numbers than ever before; and where it is deemed necessary to silence the voice of opposition, blocks of railroad stocks are bestowed in liberal quantities. In every state where railroad commissions have been established, they have proved to be dead failures. Where a determined stand has been taken against encroachments of railroads by a commission, the courts have set aside the verdict of the commissioners. Where the property of the railroad has been threatened by a commission, the railroads have taken the precaution to add the railroad commissioners to their assets. Wherever that could not be done, the court has been knocked down to the railroad, and opposition has been silenced through legal decisions. Everywhere, and in all ages, the people have at first accepted compromises; they have not pressed for radical measures of relief until the half-way policy has failed; and it has never succeeded for any length of time, except where the people have been misled. Where the shadow has been substituted for the substance, and for a time deceived the people, they have still continued to feel the oppressions and exactions of the iron hand in one way or another, and the clamor for radical measures has broken out in tones louder than before. The Interstate Commerce Law is a half-way measure; it but lances the sore where amputation is necessary; intended to control, it is itself controlled, and the summing up of a railroad manager before the Interstate Commerce Commission clearly demonstrates the utter worthlessness of that institution. It reads:—

Rates are absolutely demoralized, and neither shippers, passengers, railways, or the public in general make anything by this state of affairs. Take passenger rates, for instance; they are very low, but who benefits by the reduction? No one but the scalpers. In freight matters the case is just the same. Certain shippers are allowed heavy rebates, while others are made to pay full rates. . . . The management is dishonest on all sides, and there is not a road in the country that can be accused of living up to the Interstate law.

Governmental control of railroads has not succeeded and never will succeed. So long as it is in the power of a board of directors to increase stocks (all water), issue bonds, and give rebates in secret, the people will have to pay for all the water and the interest on the bonds. Favors are shown to trusts and combines; the trusts and combines are made up of the directors and stockholders of the railroads; they secretly allow rebates to their favorites, such institutions as have railroad directors on the roll of stockholders having an undoubted advantage over their competitors. No system of governmental control can reach the offenders. Public control is inconsistent with the idea of private ownership, and private ownership of public institutions is not consistent with well-founded principles of public policy and welfare. Public control without public ownership is an impossibility. What the government has a right to control it has a right to own and operate. Ownership must precede control, and the question must be solved in a very short time, or those who own the railroads will own the government.

[8.]   *"Transportation Is Just as Much an Industry as . . . Steel"*

Thomas F. Woodlock, railroad editor of the *Wall Street Journal,* emphasizes the accelerated pace of consolidation. [*Report of the Industrial Commission on Transportation . . . ,* Commission's Reports Vol. IX (Washington, D. C.: United States Government Printing Office, 1901), 462-63.]

Question. (By Mr. KENNEDY.) What, in your opinion, has been the influence that has been most potent in bringing about the consolidations of railroads which are going on at such a scale in the country now?—*Answer.* Really, it was the logical outcome. The movement goes back to the enactment of the interstate-commerce law. When that law was passed the railroads found themselves without what they conceived to be their only source of strength, namely, pooling. As a matter of fact, it was not, but they thought it was, and, as you know, one by one the ground was knocked from underneath on the various other forms of organizations, in place of pooling, and when the Trans-Missouri Association's decision came the last straw was gone, and Mr. C. P. Huntington—who is generally understood to be the inventor or the crystallizer of the community-of-ownership principle—said the only way for the railroads to protect themselves at all and keep things in order and prevent discrimination in rates was for the men who owned them to run them; in other words, for the directors to direct. Now, it has always been the case that a few groups of bankers— very few of them, probably seven or eight—really were in position to control 75 per cent of the important railroad mileage of the United States. You can count up now a list of probably six or seven men or interests that control 100,000 miles of the most important mileage of the country. This is a matter of public knowledge; it is not a matter of record. Now, what these men have done is this: Take the case of the Vanderbilts and the Pennsylvania Railroad Company; some time ago the Vanderbilts and the Pennsylvania Railroad people are supposed to have gotten an agreement affecting the trunk-line situation and the anthracite situation and the soft-coal situation. There was a division of responsibility. The Pennsylvania said, "I will keep everything quiet and orderly in my bailiwick;" and the Vanderbilts said, "We will keep everything quiet in ours." That is what we all suppose took place. At all events, the trunk-line situation has been quiet, and nobody is getting knowledge, and the same is true of the soft-coal situation. It is just this one thing of cutting down business; it is not any effort, necessarily, to control. Now, there have been cases where the control idea has been rendered necessary. For instance, in the case of the Union Pacific. The Union Pacific bought the control of—substantially, I think—the Southern Pacific. Why? Because the Union Pacific was, by nature and by Congress, intended originally to form one line with the Central Pacific, but the owners of the two drifted apart, and this was the first chance they had to put the two together, and the Union Pacific people bought the Southern Pacific road simply and solely for that Central Pacific line to get a clean line through from Omaha to San Francisco.

•   •   •

Question. I take it from your reply to my former question that you believe the Supreme Court of the United States, by its decision in the trans-Missouri case, killed the practice of pooling as a practical question, and forced, in a way, the combinations which have been going on ever since in the railroads?—*Answer.* Yes; and I do not think, even if a law were passed allowing the railroads to pool, they would pool. This has been the simplest and safest solution of their trouble; in fact, the only safe solution. None of their associations were of any value. There was always some member kicking and making trouble in it. The combinations were very costly to maintain, and they were always having trouble with them. There was not one of them that worked well, not even the Trunk Line Association. There was a row there half the time. Well, all that is finished. The railroads are directed by their own directors, and these people happen to be the same directors for many of them, the effect being that if a man gets a rate or gives a rebate, and does something he ought not to, he can be reached at once.

Question. This scheme will do away with ruinous competition, and perhaps with the former trouble that brought about receiverships, etc.?—*Answer.* It will certainly tend to prevent disturbance of rates. Rates have been more stable in the United States in the last two years than they have been in the last thirty years. I guess there is no question about that. The rate situation has been absolutely peaceful compared with what it was three years ago.

Question. You look upon the community-of-interest consolidation of railroads as a good thing, then?—*Answer.* I think the community of ownership, as it is called, whereby the management of these roads is concentrated in a few hands, may in theory be a bad thing, but in practice it would not be found profitable as a bad thing. In other words, if they do not run these railroads on the principle of stability of rates, economy in management, and efficiency in running the machinery, there is no sense in it, and I am positive that that is what they have in mind.

• • •

Question. Have you anything to say on the question of Government ownership of railroads?—*Answer.* I do not think it would be good for the Government or good for the people. I do not see why the Government should own the railroads at all; I do not see any more reason for it than that the Government should go into the steel business or newspaper business. There is no essential difference between the two things. The manufacture of transportation is just as much an industry as the manufacture of steel.

II

INDUSTRY

Manufacturing, as well as communications, was transformed by a revolution in technology. Not only did the steam engine power the locomotive, it also powered thousands of other machines throughout the land. Productivity multiplied. In 1776 Adam Smith calculated that without machinery a man could make twenty common pins a day, but that with it ten laborers could manufacture more than 48,000 pins daily. A century later in Massachusetts seventy machines tended by three laborers, one machinist, and a boy turned out 7,500,000 packaged pins daily. During the Gilded Age the manufacturing production index, showing the growth of industry, rose from 17 to 100. Elaborate machinery necessitated immense capital and large-scale production required wide-spread markets. Corporations grew by eliminating rivals through cutthroat competition and by peaceful merger. By 1899 manufacturing was so consolidated that monopolistic industries—those in which the four leading corporations controlled more than one-half of the nation's total production—earned 32 per cent of the manufacturing income. Bringing order and efficiency to industry, these powerful and monopolistic "trusts," like the railroads, forced Americans to evaluate their traditional faith in individualism, competition, and *laissez faire.*

[9.] *"A Nightmare of Iron and Brass"*

The cotton press, described here by newspaper reporter and noted writer Lafcadio Hearn, is an example of the gigantic machines introduced in the Gilded Age. [Lafcadio Hearn, *The Commercial* (Cincinnati), November 26, 1877, in Lafcadio Hearn, *Occidental Gleanings,* ed. Albert Mordell (New York: Dodd, Mead & Company, 1925), I, 171-74. Reprinted by permission of Dodd, Mead & Company.]

I have just witnessed a terrible exhibition of the power of machinery. Friends had advised me to visit the huge cotton press at the Cotton Landing, and I spent several hours in watching its operation. Excepting, perhaps, some of the monster cotton presses of India, it is said to be the most powerful in the world; but the East Indian presses box the cotton instead of baling it, with enormous loss of time. This "Champion" press at the New Orleans Levee weighs, with all its attachments, upwards of three thousand tons, and exerts the enormous pressure of four million pounds upon the bales placed in it. When I first arrived at the gate of the building where the machinery is placed, they were loading the newly pressed bales upon drays—bales much smaller than the ordinary plantation bales. I was considerably surprised to see three or four negroes straining with all their might to roll one of these bales; but I was not then aware that each of the packages of cotton before me weighed upward of *one thousand pounds*. They were really double—two bales pressed into one, and bound with twelve ties instead of six, and were being packed thus for shipment upon the vessel *Western Empire* for foreign parts. One of the gentlemen connected with the office kindly measured a double bale for me, with an ingenious instrument especially made for such measurements. It proved to be less than two feet through its thickest diameter—considerably less than most ordinary single bales.

The spectacle of this colossal press in motion is really terrific. It is like a nightmare of iron and brass. It does not press downward, but upward. It is not a press as we understand the term generally, but an enormous mouth of metal which seizes the bale and crushes it in its teeth. The machine did not give me the idea of a machine, it seemed rather some vast, black genie, buried up to his neck in the earth by the will of Soliman, the pre-Adamite Sultan.

Fancy a monstrous head of living iron and brass, fifty feet high from its junction with the ground, having pointed gaps in its face like gothic eyes, a mouth five feet wide, opening six feet from the mastodon teeth in the lower jaw to the mastodon teeth in the upper jaw. The lower jaw alone moves, as in living beings, and it is worked by two vast iron tendons, long and thick and solid as church pillars. The surface of this lower jaw is equivalent to six square feet.

The more I looked at the thing, the more I felt as though its prodigious anatomy had been studied after the anatomy of some extinct animal,—the way those jaws worked, the manner in which those muscles moved.

Men rolled a cotton bale to the mouth of the monster. The jaws opened with a low roar, and so remained. The lower jaw had descended to a level with the platform on which the bale was lying. It was an immense planta-

tion bale. Two black men rolled it into the yawning mouth. The titan
muscles contracted, and the jaw closed, silently, steadily, swiftly. The bale
flattened, flattened, flattened—down to sixteen inches, twelve inches, eight
inches, five inches. Positively less than five inches! I thought it was going
to disappear altogether. But after crushing it beyond five inches the jaws
remained stationary and the monster growled like rumbling thunder. I
thought the machine began to look as hideous as one of those horrible
yawning heads which formed the gates of the *teocallis* at Palenque, and
through whose awful jaws the sacrificial victims passed.

I noticed that the iron tie-bands which had been passed through the
teeth were not fastened by hand. No hand could pull them tight enough
to resist the internal pressure of the captive bale. They were fastened by
very powerful steel levers, called "pullers," which slid along a bar, and by
which the bands were pulled so tight that all the "slack" (or at least nearly
all) is taken out of the bale, and the bands cut deeply into the cotton. With
the "pullers" the strain upon the bands becomes two thousand pounds to
each band, a peculiar tie-grip being invented to insure against breaking.
The levers pull both ends of the band at the same time with the same ten-
sion.

It seemed to me evidently less than a minute from the time of feeding
the machine until the bale was rolled out, flat as a pillow, and hard as the
hardest wood. It still remained only five inches thick at the sides, but the
internal pressure bent out the bands ovally so that the bale became about
a foot thick in the center. Yet the reduction seemed magical. I am told
this machine presses upwards of six hundred bales a day. . . . Perhaps I
could not give you a better idea of the power of this machine than by stating the fact that not long ago, during a test exhibition, it compressed a bale
of good cotton to a density of *eighty pounds per cubic foot!*

[10.] *"We Were Moles*
Burrowing in the Dark"

Andrew Carnegie tells how he succeeded in iron and steel.
[Andrew Carnegie, *Autobiography of Andrew Carnegie* (Boston: Houghton Mifflin Company, 1920), pp. 135-36, 176-77,
181-84. Reprinted by permission of Houghton Mifflin Company.]

As I became acquainted with the manufacture of iron I was greatly surprised to find that the cost of each of the various processes was unknown. Inquiries made of the leading manufacturers of Pittsburgh proved this. It was a lump business, and until stock was taken and the books balanced at the end of the year, the manufacturers were in total ignorance of results. I heard of men who thought their business at the end of the year would show a loss and had found a profit, and *vice-versa*. I felt as if we were moles burrowing in the dark, and this to me was intolerable. I insisted upon such a system of weighing and accounting being introduced throughout our works as would enable us to know what our cost was for each process and especially what each man was doing, who saved material, who wasted it, and who produced the best results.

To arrive at this was a much more difficult task than one would imagine. Every manager in the mills was naturally against the new system. Years were required before an accurate system was obtained, but eventually, by the aid of many clerks and the introduction of weighing scales at various points in the mill, we began to know not only what every department was doing, but what each one of the many men working at the furnaces was doing, and thus to compare one with another. One of the chief sources of success in manufacturing is the introduction and strict maintenance of a perfect system of accounting so that responsibility for money or materials can be brought home to every man. Owners who, in the office, would not trust a clerk with five dollars without having a check upon him, were supplying tons of material daily to men in the mills without exacting an account of their stewardship by weighing what each returned in the finished form.

The Siemens Gas Furnace had been used to some extent in Great Britain for heating steel and iron, but it was supposed to be too expensive. I well remember the criticisms made by older heads among the Pittsburgh manufacturers about the extravagant expenditure we were making upon these new-fangled furnaces. But in the heating of great masses of material, almost half the waste could sometimes be saved by using the new furnaces. The expenditure would have been justified, even if it had been doubled. Yet it was many years before we were followed in this new departure; and in some of those years the margin of profit was so small that the most of it was made up from the savings derived from the adoption of the improved furnaces.

Our strict system of accounting enabled us to detect the great waste possible in heating large masses of iron. This improvement revealed to us a valuable man in a clerk, William Borntraeger, . . . who came from Germany. He surprised us one day by presenting a detailed statement showing results for a period, which seemed incredible. All the needed labor in preparing this statement he had performed at night unasked and unknown to us. The form adapted was uniquely original. Needless to say, William soon became superintendent of the works and later a partner, and the poor German lad died a millionaire. He well deserved his fortune.

●   ●   ●

. . . I had become interested, with my friends of the Pennsylvania Railroad Company, in building some railways in the Western States, but gradually withdrew from all such enterprises and made up my mind to go entirely contrary to the adage not to put all one's eggs in one basket. I determined that the proper policy was "to put all good eggs in one basket and then watch that basket."

I believe the true road to preëminent success in any line is to make yourself master in that line. I have no faith in the policy of scattering one's resources, and in my experience I have rarely if ever met a man who achieved preëminence in money-making—certainly never one in manufacturing—who was interested in many concerns. The men who have succeeded are men who have chosen one line and stuck to it. . . .

●   ●   ●

Looking back to-day it seems incredible that only forty years ago (1870) chemistry in the United States was an almost unknown agent in connection with the manufacture of pig iron. It was the agency, above all others, most needful in the manufacture of iron and steel. The blast-furnace manager of that day was usually a rude bully, generally a foreigner, who in addition to his other acquirements was able to knock down a man now and then as a lesson to the other unruly spirits under him. He was supposed to diagnose the condition of the furnace by instinct, to possess some almost supernatural power of divination, like his congener in the country districts who was reputed to be able to locate an oil well or water supply by means of a hazel rod. He was a veritable quack doctor who applied whatever remedies occurred to him for the troubles of his patient.

The Lucy Furnace was out of one trouble and into another, owing to the great variety of ores, limestone, and coke which were then supplied with little or no regard to their component parts. This state of affairs became intolerable to us. We finally decided to dispense with the rule-of-thumb-and-intuition manager, and to place a young man in charge of the furnace. We had a young shipping clerk, Henry M. Curry, who had distinguished himself, and it was resolved to make him manager.

●   ●   ●

The next step taken was to find a chemist as Mr. Curry's assistant and guide. We found the man in a learned German, Dr. Fricke, and great secrets did the doctor open up to us. Iron stone from mines that had a high reputation was now found to contain ten, fifteen, and even twenty per cent less iron than it had been credited with. Mines that hitherto had a poor reputation we found to be now yielding superior ore. The good was bad and the bad was good, and everything was topsy-turvy. Nine tenths of all the uncertainties of pig-iron making were dispelled under the burning sun of chemical knowledge.

At a most critical period when it was necessary for the credit of the firm that the blast furnace should make its best product, it had been stopped because an exceedingly rich and pure ore had been substituted for an inferior ore—an ore which did not yield more than two thirds of the quantity of iron of the other. The furnace had met with disaster because too much lime had been used to flux this exceptionally pure ironstone. The very superiority of the materials had involved us in serious losses.

What fools we had been! But then there was this consolation: we were not as great fools as our competitors. It was years after we had taken chemistry to guide us that it was said by the proprietors of some other furnaces that they could not afford to employ a chemist. Had they known the truth then, they would have known that they could not afford to be without one. Looking back it seems pardonable to record that we were the first to employ a chemist at blast furnaces—something our competitors pronounced extravagant.

The Lucy Furnace became the most profitable branch of our business, because we had almost the entire monopoly of scientific management. Having discovered the secret, it was not long (1872) before we decided to erect an additional furnace. This was done with great economy as compared with our first experiment. The mines which had no reputation and the products of which many firms would not permit to be used in their blast furnaces found a purchaser in us. Those mines which were able to obtain an enormous price for their products, owing to a reputation for quality, we quietly ignored. A curious illustration of this was the celebrated Pilot Knob mine in Missouri. Its product was, so to speak, under a cloud. A small portion of it only could be used, it was said, without obstructing the furnace. Chemistry told us that it was low in phosphorus, but very high in silicon. There was no better ore and scarcely any as rich, if it were properly fluxed. We therefore bought heavily of this and received the thanks of the proprietors for rendering their property valuable.

It is hardly believable that for several years we were able to dispose of the highly phosphoric cinder from the puddling furnaces at a higher price than we had to pay for the pure cinder from the heating furnaces of our competitors—a cinder which was richer in iron than the puddled cinder and much freer from phosphorus. Upon some occasion a blast furnace had attempted to smelt the flue cinder, and from its greater purity the furnace did not work well with a mixture intended for an impurer article; hence for years it was thrown over the banks of the river at Pittsburgh by our competitors as worthless. In some cases we were even able to exchange a poor article for a good one and obtain a bonus.

But it is still more unbelievable that a prejudice, equally unfounded, existed against putting into the blast furnaces the roll-scale from the mills which was pure oxide of iron. This reminds me of my dear friend and fellow-Dunfermline townsman, Mr. Chisholm, of Cleveland. We had many pranks together. One day, when I was visiting his works at Cleveland, I saw men wheeling this valuable roll-scale into the yard. I asked Mr. Chisholm where they were going with it, and he said:

"To throw it over the bank. Our managers have always complained that they had bad luck when they attempted to remelt it in the blast furnace."

I said nothing, but upon my return to Pittsburgh I set about having a joke at his expense. We had then a young man in our service named Du Puy, whose father was known as the inventor of a direct process in iron-making with which he was then experimenting in Pittsburgh. I recommended our people to send Du Puy to Cleveland to contract for all the roll-scale of my friend's establishment. He did so, buying it for fifty cents per ton and having it shipped to him direct. This continued for some time. I expected always to hear of the joke being discovered. The premature death of Mr. Chisholm occurred before I could apprise him of it. His successors soon, however, followed our example.

[11.] *"An Unbroken Chorus of Protests"*

Henry D. Lloyd, an early muckraker, lists "the various meta-morphoses through which" the men of Standard Oil "have passed" and claims that as late as 1897 the practice of shipping discriminations flourished "as rankly as it ever did." [Henry D. Lloyd, "The Oil Combination," *The Independent* (New York), Vol. XLIX, No. 2518 (March 4, 1897), 266-67.]

The "Standard Oil Trust" is one of a series of names which the men who have obtained the power to fix the price of the "light of the world" have taken in the various metamorphoses through which they have passed in their evolution from poor boys to richest men. Not to recite them all, the first investiture of importance was under the name of the Standard Oil Company in 1870. In 1872, still keeping this name, they put on the dress of the famous South Improvement Company; in 1882 they formed the Standard Oil Trust; in 1892, they announced the dissolution of the trust as having been "begun"; in 1897 the dissolution is still in progress. In the case of natural persons, as the law calls ordinary men and women, the process of dissolution is attended by grief, decay and disappearance. When Lazarus had been dead only four days his physical condition, according to Martha, was most unpleasant. But the artificial person, the corporation or the combination of corporations, the trust, is superior to these disabilities of the living. The trust, altho these five years in the agonies of dissolution, has been never happier or more prosperous. Its dividends have never been larger; the quotations of its stock have never been higher. While it was alive, its stock sold as high as 185; now that it is dead, the papers chronicle an advance during the week just past from 265½ to 279¼. While it was alive, the dividends it paid were stated by the President to the New York Legislature to be 10 per cent. a year on its $90,000,000 of stock, besides a stock bonus of 3 or 4 per cent. But when dead, or in dissolution, in 1896, its dividends are over 30 per cent., and the capital is now stated to be $97,000,000. A press dispatch, dated New York, February 12th, gives notice that the trustees will pay for the last quarter of 1896 the regular dividend of 3 per cent. and a bonus of 7 per cent., making a total dividend of nearly $10,000,000 in cash to be paid for the last three months of 1896. Evidently, the stockholders of this dissolving trust are not suffering from any neuralgia of what Dr. Rainsford has called "the nerve of discontent."

Whatever may be the "label" which the owners of the vast aggregation of refineries, pipe lines, oil wells, and other agencies that dominate the petroleum market may choose to give it, the fact is not even questioned that it still remains under a common ownership and is still directed by a common purpose—the control of a great necessary of life—and the quotations of its stock and the dividends paid are the evidence of how unbroken is still the success which has now lasted for a quarter of a century.

The Americans are a competitive people. They are devoted to business, making money, developing the resources of the country; and they are a chivalrous and generous people, always rejoicing in the victories of those runners of the race for wealth who have won the right to wear the crown that all were striving for. Why is it that the success of the group of men who have under different names in the oil business achieved the greatest fortunes that have ever, in the history of commerce, been got in one generation has excited from the beginning till now without cessation an un-

broken chorus of protests, investigations by the States and the nation, law-
suits, private and public, condemnations by the courts, State and national,
civil and criminal, and uprisings of the people in all forms from incipient
civil war in the oil regions to the exercise of their highest sovereignty by
the amendment of the constitutions of sixteen States to prevent trusts?
Has the character of the American people changed to a sordid and mean
enviousness or have the methods of business changed?

As is shown by the testimony taken by the Committee of the New York
Legislature, which investigated this subject in 1879 at the instance of the
New York Chamber of Commerce, and by the House of Representatives
Committee on Manufactures in 1888, the men who organized this brilliant
financial success in oil, were neither capitalists, nor oil discoverers, nor oil
experts in any branch. They began with nothing, as one of their lawyers
said of one of them in court. They had less capital, the New York Legislature found, than the competitors whom they drove out of business. They
were not the ones to "strike oil." Long after their trust was formed they
owned only a very small part of the oil lands; their success was not due to
their being the discoverers or owners of "gushers." No modern industry
has gone with such leaps from primitive methods to the most highly developed mechanical perfection as that of oil; but these leaders of the trust
did not invent nor introduce one of these improved processes—neither the
pipe line nor the tank car nor the drill or still. If the quotations just given
for the stock represent actual sales—and they are justified by the earnings
cited—the stock exchange value of the trust is in round numbers over
$225,000,000. The men who had "nothing" in the early sixties now have
the control of this fabulous sum in oil alone. The trust is a combination of
corporations—a score or more. Hundreds of corporations all over the world
have been condensed to make this score. Perhaps this lubrication of poverty
into almost unaccountable millions is a triumph of co-operation. One of its
members in a public defense has described it as an instance of what can
be done by "voluntary co-operation." But the records show, on the sworn
testimony of the organizers of the combination, that substantially the same
men own the majority of this vast aggregation as began with nothing, and
then formed the Standard Oil Company in 1870 with one million dollars
capital. It has been a little group of less than a dozen men, owning more
than half of practically every concern in the combination, as individuals;
and there is a group within the group. "A majority of the stock being
held by four men," the lawyer of the trust was reported in the New York
papers to have said at the time of the dissolution in 1892. The trustees have
been "co-operating," but the hundreds, thousands, of capitalists, inventors,
pioneers, merchants, manufacturers, oil-well owners, who have surrendered

the whole or the control of their business and passed out of sight or into the minority, were entirely unaware that they were participants in a "voluntary co-operation," if the clamor they have made for justice for thirty years before the courts, Legislatures and the bar of public opinion is in evidence.

"Co-operation" was not the secret of this success, but was itself the result of the secret of success, whatever that was. What was it that the successful men had which their competitors, tho they had more capital and every process of refining and every legitimate advantage, had not? Their competitors had all things, said the New York legislative committee of 1878, "save their ability to acquire facilities for transportation." When one of the trust was asked by the New York Legislature in 1888 if its members had not had better freight rates than their competitors he "could not recall anything of the kind." But the charges that certain members of the trust made secret agreements with the officials of the railroads by which their competitors were driven out of business by extortionate rates—the railroads even agreeing to pay over to these members of the trust the extortionate sums they thus collected from the unsuspecting rivals—have been laboriously tried by the Legislatures and courts, State and national, for over a quarter of a century, and their truth has been placed beyond the possibility of denial. The Inter-State Commerce Act was passed in 1887 to make the detection and punishment of this always illegal wrong easier; but the Inter-State Commission found, as late as 1893, that certain members of the oil combination were getting discriminations from the railroads that were "wholly indefensible," "obnoxious," "inexcusable," "gross," "most unjust and injurious."

•   •   •

The gentlemen who were receiving the benefit of such rates and helping to build up "nothing" into the control of $225,000,000 in thirty years, denied that they were receiving them when, as the New York Legislature and the Supreme Court of Ohio and the Inter-State Commerce Commission have decided, they were getting them, and getting them on a scale to ruin their competitors. Are they now violating the law and receiving special and secret favors? There is no adjudicated evidence; the victims finding that the decisions of the courts did them no good have stopped going to the courts. But no man of affairs doubts that the practice of discriminations on the railroads still flourishes as rankly as it ever did.

[12.] *"Random Reminiscences"*

John D. Rockefeller recalls life with father and the question of rebates. [John D. Rockefeller, *Random Reminiscences of Men and Events* (New York: Doubleday, Page & Company, [now Doubleday & Company, Inc.], 1909), pp. 33, 46-47, 107-09, 111-12. © 1909 by Doubleday & Co., Inc., renewed 1936 by John D. Rockefeller. Reprinted by permission of the Trustees of the trust created for Margaret Strong De Cuevas under the Will of John D. Rockefeller.]

To my father I owe a great debt in that he himself trained me to practical ways. He was engaged in different enterprises; he used to tell me about these things, explaining their significance; and he taught me the principles and methods of business. From early boyhood I kept a little book which I remember I called Ledger A—and this little volume is still preserved—containing my receipts and expenditures as well as an account of the small sums that I was taught to give away regularly.

•   •   •

My loans from my father were many. Our relations on finances were a source of some anxiety to me, and were not quite so humorous as they seem now as I look back at them. Occasionally he would come to me and say that if I needed money in the business he would be able to loan some, and as I always needed capital I was glad indeed to get it, even at 10 per cent. interest. Just at the moment when I required the money most he was apt to say:

"My son, I find I have got to have that money."

"Of course, you shall have it at once," I would answer, but I knew that he was testing me, and that when I paid him, he would hold the money without its earning anything for a little time, and then offer it back later. I confess that this little discipline should have done me good, and perhaps did, but while I concealed it from him, the truth is I was not particularly pleased with his application of tests to discover if my financial ability was equal to such shocks.

•   •   •

The Question of Rebates

Of all the subjects which seem to have attracted the attention of the public to the affairs of the Standard Oil Company, the matter of rebates from railroads has perhaps been uppermost. The Standard Oil Company of Ohio, of which I was president, did receive rebates from the railroads prior to 1880, but received no advantages for which it did not give full compensation. The reason for rebates was that such was the railroads' method of business. A public rate was made and collected by the railroad companies, but, so far as my knowledge extends, was seldom retained in full; a portion of it was repaid to the shippers as a rebate. By this method the real rate of freight which any shipper paid was not known by his competitors nor by other railroad companies, the amount being a matter of bargain with the carrying company. Each shipper made the best bargain that he could, but whether he was doing better than his competitor was only a matter of conjecture. Much depended upon whether the shipper had the advantage of competition of carriers.

The Standard Oil Company of Ohio, being situated at Cleveland, had the advantage of different carrying lines, as well as of water transportation in the summer; taking advantage of those facilities, it made the best bargains possible for its freights. Other companies sought to do the same. The Standard gave advantages to the railroads for the purpose of reducing the cost of transportation of freight. It offered freights in large quantity, car-loads and train-loads. It furnished loading facilities and discharging facilities at great cost. It provided regular traffic, so that a railroad could conduct its transportation to the best advantage and use its equipment to the full extent of its hauling capacity without waiting for the refiner's convenience. It exempted railroads from liability for fire and carried its own insurance. It provided at its own expense terminal facilities which permitted economies in handling. For these services it obtained contracts for special allowances on freights.

But notwithstanding these special allowances, this traffic from the Standard Oil Company was far more profitable to the railroad companies than the smaller and irregular traffic, which might have paid a higher rate.

• • •

The profits of the Standard Oil Company did not come from advantages given by railroads. The railroads, rather, were the ones who profited by the traffic of the Standard Oil Company, and whatever advantage it received in its constant efforts to reduce rates of freight was only one of the many elements of lessening cost to the consumer which enabled us to increase our volume of business the world over because we could reduce the selling price.

How general was the complicated bargaining for rates can hardly be imagined; everyone got the best rate that he could. . . . I well remember a bright man from Boston who had much to say about rebates and drawbacks. He was an old and experienced merchant, and looked after his affairs with a cautious and watchful eye. He feared that some of his competitors were doing better than he in bargaining for rates, and he delivered himself of this conviction:

"I am opposed on principle to the whole system of rebates and drawbacks—unless I am in it."

[13.] *"The Last Thing To Do Is To Legislate"*

William Graham Sumner of Yale University explains the doctrine of *laissez faire*. [William Graham Sumner, *Essays of William Graham Sumner,* ed. Albert Galloway Keller and Maurice R. Davie (New Haven: Yale University Press, 1934), II, 472-75. Reprinted by permission of the publisher.]

The doctrine and precept of *laissez-faire* do not preclude the attainment of positive results from investigation, nor the formulation of accurate statements of those results, nor the most elaborate verification of those results. The students of the *laissez-faire* school have done nearly all that ever has yet been done in the way of actual achievement under all these heads. *Laissez-faire* means: Do not meddle; wait and observe. Do not regulate; study. Do not give orders; be teachable. Do not enter upon any rash experiments; be patient until you see how it will work out.

The contrary temper is plainly manifested in our day on every hand. A man who has studied into any social question far enough to be nonplussed by its difficulties will propose some form of legislation about it. *Laissez-faire* would teach: At this time and under such a state of the question, the last thing to do is to legislate about it. When a half-dozen large and delicate interests are involved in a matter like transportation, in such a way that no human intelligence can possibly comprehend and adjust them, least of all by a piece of legislation which must be inelastic and arbitrary, this state of things is made a reason, not for letting the matter alone, but for passing some legislation by way of experiment. Nothing could reveal more astoundingly the prevailing ignorance of what a society is and what methods of dealing with it are rational; for it is not possible to experiment with a society and just drop the experiment whenever we choose. The experiment enters into the life of the society and never can be got out again. Therefore, whenever there is a mania for interference, the doctrine of non-interference is the highest wisdom. . . .

• • •

. . . The greatest obstacle to any rational and true social improvement at this moment is the well-founded alarm excited by every proposition to do something by legislation—which compels all sober men to insist upon *laissez-faire* as an absolute principle of safety. In the face of those who are elaborating a social policy for us, there is often nothing to do but prevent anything from being done. Nearly all the machinery of Congress is an elaborate mechanism for preventing anything from being done, and although it stops many measures which a great many of us might think it very advisable to pass, we cheerfully do without them lest some of the others should get through likewise. The only fault with the mechanism is that it is not perfect enough. It fails when there is great clamor out of doors, for there is always cowardice inside, and then a Bland Bill or something of that sort can get a two-thirds vote and rise above the barrier of obstruction.

[14.] *"The True Function of Government"*

Lester F. Ward, an experienced civil servant and an outstanding sociologist, observes "the failure of government to keep pace with . . . change." [Lester F. Ward, "Plutocracy and Paternalism," *The Forum*, XX, No. 3 (November 1895), 304.]

From this point of view, then, modern society is suffering from the very opposite of paternalism,—from under-government, from the failure of government to keep pace with the change which civilization has wrought in substituting intellectual for physical qualities as the workers of injustice. Government to-day is powerless to perform its primary and original function of protecting society. There was a time when brigandage stalked abroad throughout Europe and no one was safe in life or property. This was due to lack of adequate government. Man's nature has not changed, but brigandage has succumbed to the strong arm of the law. Human rapacity now works in subtler ways. Plutocracy is the modern brigandage and can be dislodged only by the same power, —the power of the state. All the evils of society are the result of the free flow of natural propensities. The purpose of government is, as far as may be, to prevent this from causing injustice. The physical passions of men are natural and healthy, but they cannot be allowed to go unbridled. Government was established, not to lessen or even to alter them. Exactly the same is needed to be done with the higher acquisitive faculty. It need not be condemned; it cannot be suppressed: but it can and should be directed into harmless ways and restricted to useful purposes. Properly viewed, too, this is to secure its maximum exercise and greatest freedom, for unrestrained license soon leads to conflict, chokes its own free operation, and puts an end to its activity. The true function of government is not to fetter but to liberate the forces of society, not to diminish but to increase their effectiveness. Unbridled competition destroys itself. The only competition that endures is that which goes on under judicious regulation.

[15.] *"As Brilliant . . . a Gathering as Ever Assembled in Chicago"*

The Chicago Conference on Trusts seeks answers to the problems caused by the consolidation of industry. [*Chicago Conference on Trusts* (Chicago: The Civic Federation of Chicago, 1900), p. 451.]

. . . By 7 o'clock State street was packed with a struggling crowd working toward the doors of the hall where the conference was to convene an hour later, and when Chairman Howe's gavel fell at 8 o'clock the auditorium was packed from the parquette to the outside edge of the upper gallery and there were ten thousand people clamoring in the street for admission. The boxes were filled with a brilliant audience of society people, and the delegates made way in their seats for scores of gaily dressed women, while the aisles were utilized to accommodate as much of the overflow as possible. Altogether the audience was as brilliant and intellectual a gathering as ever assembled in Chicago, and bore testimony to the interest of all classes in the question under debate.

[16.] *"When Dreyfus Shall Have Been Forgotten"*

A paragraph from reformer William Dudley Foulke's speech expresses the delegates' sense of mission. [*Chicago Conference on Trusts*, p. 452.]

The question we are called to consider dwarfs in importance all other issues now before the country or the world. When Dreyfus shall have been forgotten, when the war in the Philippines shall be regarded only as one of the episodes of history, when men shall speak no longer of the tariff or the currency, the present era may well be remembered by coming generations as the epoch of that great organic change when the system of competition began to give way to the system of co-operation—a change leading inevitably (whether for good or ill we cannot clearly see) to the radical reconstruction of the world's industrial and social life.

[17.] *"To Put Rings in the Noses of Hogs"*

William Jennings Bryan, titular leader of the Democratic party, claims that the function of government is to keep "hoggish" people from trespassing "upon the rights of others." [*Chicago Conference on Trusts*, pp. 497-98, 500-501, 510-12.]

I want to start with the declaration that a monopoly in private hands is indefensible from any standpoint, and intolerable. I make no exceptions to the rule. I do not divide monopolies in private hands into good monopolies and bad monopolies. There is no good monopoly in private hands. There can be no good monopoly in private hands until the Almighty sends us angels to preside over the monopoly. There may be a despot who is better than another despot, but there is no good despotism. One trust may be less harmful than another. One trust magnate may be more benevolent than another, but there is no good monopoly in private hands, and I do not believe it is safe for society to permit any man or group of men to monopolize any article of merchandise or any branch of industry.

What is the defense made of the monopoly? The defense of the monopoly is always placed on the ground that if you will allow a few people to control the market and fix the price they will be good to the people who purchase of them. The entire defense of the trusts rests upon a money argument. If the trust will sell to a man an article for a dollar less than the article will cost under other conditions, then in the opinion of some that proves a trust to be a good thing. In the first place I deny that under a monopoly the price will be reduced. In the second place, if under a monopoly the price is reduced the objections to a monopoly from other standpoints far outweigh any financial advantage that the trust could bring. But I protest in the beginning against settling every question upon the dollar argument. I protest against the attempt to drag every question down to the low level of dollars and cents.

In 1859 Abraham Lincoln wrote a letter to the Republicans of Boston who were celebrating Jefferson's birthday, and in the course of the letter he said: "The Republican party believes in the man and the dollar, but in case of conflict it believes in the man before the dollar." In the early years of his administration he sent a message to Congress, and in that message he warned his countryman against the approach of monarchy. And what was it that alarmed him? He said it was the attempt to put capital upon an equal footing with, if not above, labor in the structure of government, and in that attempt to put capital even upon an equal footing with labor in the structure of government he saw the approach of monarchy. Lincoln was right. Whenever you put capital upon an equal footing with labor, or above labor in the structure of government you are on the road toward a government that rests not upon reason but upon force.

Nothing is more important than that we shall in the beginning rightly understand the relation between money and man. Man is the creature of God and money is the creature of man. Money is made to be the servant of man, and I protest against all theories that enthrone money and debase mankind.

∙   ∙   ∙

What is the first thing to be expected of a trust? That it will cut down expenses. What is the second? That it will raise prices. We have not had in this country a taste of a complete trust, a complete monopoly, and we cannot tell what will be the results of a complete monopoly by looking at the results that have followed from an attempt to secure a monopoly. A corporation may lower prices to rid itself of competitors; but when it has rid itself of competitors, what is going to be the result? My friends, all you have to know is human nature. God made men selfish. . . . Occasionally I find a man who says he is not selfish, but when I do, I find a man who can prove it only by his own affidavit.

We get ideas from every source. . . . We get them from our fellow men. We get them from inanimate nature. We get them from the animals about us. I got a valuable idea once from some hogs. I was riding through Iowa and saw some hogs rooting in a field. The first thought that came to me was that those hogs were destroying a great deal in value, and then my mind ran back to the time when I lived upon a farm and when we had hogs.

Then I thought of the way in which we used to protect property from the hogs by putting rings in the noses of the hogs; and then the question came to me, why did we do it? Not to keep the hogs from getting fat, for we were more interested in their getting fat than they were; the sooner they got fat the sooner we killed them; the longer they were in getting fat the longer they lived. But why did we put the rings in their noses? So that while they were getting fat they would not destroy more than they were worth. And then the thought came to me that one of the great purposes of government was to put rings in the noses of hogs. I don't mean to say anything offensive, but we are all hoggish. In hours of temptation we are likely to trespass upon the rights of others.

I believe in self-government. I believe in the doctrines that underlie this government; I believe that people are capable of governing themselves. Why? Because in their sober moments they have helped to put rings in their own noses, to protect others from themselves and themselves from others in hours of temptation. And so I believe we must recognize human nature. We must recognize selfishness and we must so make our laws that people shall not be permitted to trespass upon the rights of others in their efforts to secure advantages for themselves.

•   •   •

. . . Every trust rests upon a corporation, and every corporation is a creature of law. The corporation is a man-made man.

When God made man as the climax of creation he looked upon his work and said that it was good, and yet when God finished his work the tallest man was not much taller than the shortest, and the strongest man was not much stronger than the weakest. That was God's plan. We looked upon his work and said that it was not quite as good as it might be, and so we made a fictitious person called a corporation that is in some instances a hundred times—a thousand times—a million times stronger than the God-made man. Then we started this man-made giant out among the God-made men. When God made man he placed a limit to his existence, so that if he was a bad man he could not do harm long, but when we made our man-made man we raised the limit as to age. In some states a corporation is given perpetual life.

When God made man he breathed into him a soul and warned him that in the next world he would be held accountable for the deeds done in the flesh, but when we made our man-made man we did not give him a soul, and if he can avoid punishment in this world he need not worry about the hereafter.

My contention is that the government that created must retain control, and that the man-made man must be admonished: "Remember now thy Creator in the days of thy youth"—and throughout thy entire life.

Let me call your attention again to this distinction. We are not dealing with the natural man; we are not dealing with natural rights. We are dealing with the man-made man and artificial privileges.

What government gives, the government can take away. What the government creates, it can control; and I insist that both the state government and the federal government must protect the God-made man from the man-made man.

●   ●   ●

I may be in error, but, in my judgment, a government of the people, by the people, and for the people, will be impossible when a few men control all the sources of production and dole out daily bread to all the rest on such terms as the few may prescribe. I believe that this nation is the hope of the world. I believe that the Declaration of Independence was the grandest document ever penned by human hands. The truths of that declaration are condensed into four great propositions: That all men are created equal; that they are endowed with inalienable rights; that governments are instituted among men to preserve those rights, and that governments derive their just powers from the consent of the governed. Such a government is impossible under an industrial aristocracy. Place the food and clothing, all that we eat and wear and use, in the hands of a few people, and instead of it being a government of the people, it will be a government of the syndicates, by the syndicates, and for the syndicates. Establish such a government, and the people will soon be powerless to secure a legislative remedy for any abuse. Establish such a system, and on the night before election the employees will be notified not to come back on the day after election unless the trusts' candidate is successful. Establish such a government, and instead of giving the right of suffrage to the people, you will virtually give the right of suffrage to the heads of monopolies, with each man empowered to vote as many times as he has employees. I am not willing to place the laboring men of this country absolutely at the mercy of the heads of monopolies. I am not willing to place the men who produce the raw material absolutely in the hands of the monopolies.

[18.] *"Has This Octopus ... Taken Possession?"*

Tammany orator W. Bourke Cockran questions Bryan's assumption that there are "oppressive monopolies." [*Chicago Conference on Trusts*, pp. 586-91.]

I agree with Mr. Bryan that if there be an oppressive monopoly in existence it should be suppressed, whatever may be the measures necessary to overthrow it. No constitutional limitation, no abstract theory of government, no mere human device, can deprive this people of the power to redress a wrong, when the existence of that wrong is clearly established.

The first question to which I think the attention of this conference should be directed is whether an oppressive monopoly exists, and if so, where it is. Before undertaking to discuss remedies we should make sure that evils exist. If their existence be established, the first step toward their redress is to define them in terms which everybody can understand. To call an industrial organization—a combine—a hydra-headed monster— or even an octopus—does not cast any light upon what it is, or illumine my pathway in attempting to deal with it.

I said yesterday that I have been suffering through every portion of this discussion from that dangerous intoxication of phrases which seems sufficient to maintain magnificent periods, but leaves us when all is over in such a state of mental bewilderment that we don't quite know what we have been talking about. I can understand how these phrases often produce great effect. Nothing frightens people so much as incomprehensible noises. Let an unaccountable noise be heard here now, and in a second we would all be trying to escape by the windows. Men may be put to intellectual as well as physical flight by the terrifying influences of sound. If, however, we are to succeed in making any recommendation of the slightest value to our fellow citizens we must at the outset compose our nerves and endeavor by the use of plain language to ascertain the precise nature of our industrial condition. Are we prosperous, or are we suffering? Is anybody injured, and by whom? Has this octopus of which we hear so much taken possession of anybody or anything? On whom or on what is it preying? Where is its lair?

To a very great extent these questions have been answered in the course of these proceedings. Representatives of labor organizations have told us from this platform that wages are higher than ever before. Certainly, these laborers do not appear to suffer from any form of oppression. But when we are about to express gratification at these comforting tidings, we are warned in solemn but mystical language that we are seeking to "place the dollar above the man." Now, what in the name of common sense can be the function of the dollar except to improve the condition of the man? Again, when we seek to ascertain the effect of corporate organizations on production, that is to say, on prosperity, we are told that a "God-made man" is one thing, and a "man-made man" is another; that the "God-made man" possesses in large degree the attributes of divinity, while the "man-made man" seems to have escaped from his creator, and to have developed habits of depravity during the separation. If this statement embodied a profound truth I am at a loss to understand what light it could throw on the question before us. We are discussing the effects, not the sources of corporate existence. But as matter of fact, is there such a thing as a "God-made man" in the world? There is, but he is scarce and rapidly growing scarcer. Why, the "God-made man" is the original savage.

Do you suppose that the oration delivered by Mr. Bryan this morning, or the rhetoric with which he moves multitudes to wild enthusiasm in every part of this country, could be evolved from the natural resources of man? The education which fits him for the platform, the books which he has read, the very clothes that he wears, have all been contributed to him by other men. He is, himself, at once a divine creation and a human development. In his natural abilities and disposition he is a "God-made man" and a credit to his creator; in his acquirements and in his extraordinary influence he is, thank heaven, a splendid type of the "man-made man."

. . . But, I repeat, what is the evil of which gentlemen here complain? The chief cause of alarm seems to be fear that competition will be stifled, yet the natural, nay, the inevitable result of competition, is the object of their most vehement denunciations. I confess I am at a loss to understand the mental processes which lead men to laud competition and yet to condemn the fruit which competition must always bear. Do you want competition, or do you not?

A Voice. Yes, we want competition.—[Mr. Cockran.] Yes, you want competition. There is a very frank man, who, I believe, agrees in the main with the proposition of Mr. Bryan. He wants competition. Can you have competition without competitors? If there be competition must not somebody succeed in it? If one competitor far excells all others, will not that excellence constitute a monopoly? Will you suppress competition when it develops unapproachable merit? Will you place limits upon excellency?

A Voice. We object to the railroads being used for the benefit of one set of fellows to the detriment of another. That is a monopoly.—*Mr. Cockran.* I agree with you there. I would invoke all the power of government to prevent that abuse and to suppress any monopoly built on it or on any form of government favor. But for the same reason that I would suppress the monopoly built on favor, I would protect the monopoly created by excellence. There is no way to suppress a monopoly arising from conspicuous merit except by the suppression of merit. If the producer of the best commodity may not dominate the market for that particular article, neither should the possessor of particular ability in any other department of human endeavor. Must we place restrictions on capacity in law and medicine, so as to place the capable and the incapable on a common level? Must we prohibit the competent lawyer from being more successful in his advocacy than his incompetent brother? Must we prevent the experienced physician from being more efficient in checking disease and relieving pain than the beginner who has just hung out his shingle?

Mr. Bryan's position, as he states it, is that monopoly in private hands is always oppressive. Instead of distinguishing between corporations which dominate the market by excellence and those dominating it by favor, he appears to distinguish between those which are successful and those which are not.

The concern which has never been able to extend its trade beyond the limits of one locality he would not molest, while, as I understand it, his plan would practically exclude by a system of federal licenses the most prosperous industries from inter-state commerce, merely because they have succeeded in the field of competition—whether that success was due to merit or favor. This would be ruinous to them, but it would also prevent the vast body of consumers from enjoying the most efficient service and the cheapest goods. . . .

A Voice. Do you contend that all the dominating industrial forces of

to-day have secured that superiority from fair competition?—*Mr. Cockran.*
No, sir. As I said last night at some length,—perhaps at such length as
to make it obscure,—some industries dominate the market through the
merit of their products established by free competition, while others control it with products of inferior merit through government favor. Any
industry maintaining a domination or monopoly of the market by the aid
of government, direct or indirect, whether extended through favors
granted by corporations exercising public franchises or through tariff
laws, is necessarily an oppressive monopoly, because if it could flourish
beyond all others through the excellency of its service, it would not need
government favor and would not accept it.

For the same reason that free competition leads to the domination of
the best, restricted competition leads to the domination of the baser, if
not of the basest.

•   •   •

We seem to have drifted into an atmosphere of bewildering vagueness
concerning what is called the evil of monopoly. I repeat if there be an
evil pressing on the necks of people, whatever its source, I am ready to
enlist under any banner to suppress it. If the Constitution stand in the
way of redressing it, then I say let us smash the Constitution and from
its fragments let us fashion weapons for the overthrow of the oppressor.
If corporate organization be an evil thing, if you can show me an evil
flowing out of it and inseparable from it, I would not hesitate a moment
to adopt Mr. Bryan's remedy. But when it is admitted, as Mr. Bryan
admitted this morning, that these evils of monopoly have not yet become
apparent,—that they are evils anticipated, not suffered,—why, then, I
say to him or to anybody who agrees with him, you are simply exciting
yourself over a fanciful picture of your own creation. Your excessive
affection for your fellows has conjured up a host of evils existing only in
your own brain. You are constituting yourself a knight errant of political
economy,—endangering the peace and prosperity of men by well-meant
but foolish attempts to redress imaginary wrongs,—not,—it is true,—
like Don Quixote tilting against windmills, but attempting to enlist the
windmills on your side.

The change which has come over this world within the last ten years
is the great phenomenon of civilization. A dozen years ago none but the
largest cities contained public parks. The pleasure grounds laid out at the
public expense, and the drives which led to them, were fully available
only to those who owned their own carriages. To-day every town of considerable size possesses its place of recreation, while every mechanic
and laborer can use the driveways on a bicycle of his own. The journey

to and from the place of labor which formerly the laborer made every day at a snail's pace in wretched street cars, with spluttering oil lamps, drawn by miserable horses or mules, is made to-day in rapid comfortable vehicles, lighted and moved by electricity. Every workman is better housed, earns higher wages, eats more abundant and more wholesome food, reads more books and better books than ever before in the history of the race. Everywhere we find the masses of the people entering into the possession of their own, showing by the ruddier flush of health on their cheeks and the increased efficiency of their arms that God Almighty is guiding the race forward and upward,—that the height which man has reached is not a dizzy eminence from which he will fall back to disaster, but solid ground from which he will rise to still wider prosperity.

When we realize that this is an age of marvelous improvement, that the conditions of men are growing better and better every day, we ought to hesitate a while before we change the industrial system evolved from experience, for fanciful experiments suggested by exuberant rhetoric.

III

THE FARM

Thomas Jefferson's ideal, the small independent farmer, became obsolete in the Gilded Age. Hard work, poor compensation, isolation, and primitive living conditions drove many off the farm. In addition, a profound revolution in agricultural technology transformed farming. Costly machinery, and more acreage to utilize it fully, increased production—but also increased the farmer's debts. To pay these debts, farmers shunned diversification and specialized in cash crops. Specialization in turn made the farmer more dependent upon the marketplace. Blindly competing among themselves, farmers were no match for the better organized, consolidated and monopolized sectors of the economy. They mortgaged their farms on bankers' terms, paid railroads exorbitant rates to transport their products while they purchased their supplies, and sold their crops at prices dictated by middlemen. The more fortunate farmers expanded their holdings and became firmly enmeshed in the mechanism of the marketplace. The less fortunate ones moved to the city or maintained a marginal existence as small independent farmers, tenant farmers, or farm laborers.

[19.] *"I Doubt If There Is Greater Liberality Shown to Laborers"*

John C. Calhoun, an Arkansas planter and grandson of the statesman, gives the proprietor's view of Negro farm labor. [Senate Committee on Education and Labor, *The Relations Between Labor and Capital* . . . (Washington, D. C.: United States Government Printing Office, 1885), II, 158-61.]

Question 1. What is the condition of the laborers in your section?—
Answer. The laborers in the Mississippi Valley are agricultural. But few
whites are employed; they soon become land-owners or tenants. Your
question, therefore, reduces itself to, What is the condition of the negroes?
I should say good, as compared with a few years ago, and improving.
You must recollect that it has only been 18 years since the negroes emerged
from slavery without a dollar and with no education, and that for generations they had been taught to rely entirely upon others for guidance
and support. They became, therefore, at once the easy prey of unscrupulous
men, who used them for their personal aggrandizement, were subjected
to every evil influence, and did not discover for years the impositions
practiced upon them. They were indolent and extravagant, and eager to
buy on a credit everything the planter or merchant would sell them. The
planter had nothing except the land, which, with the crop to be grown,
was mortgaged generally for advances. If he refused to indulge his laborers
in extravagant habits during the year, by crediting them for articles not
absolutely necessary, his action was regarded as good grounds for them
to quit work, and there were those present who were always ready to
use this as an argument to array the negroes against the proprietors. This,
of course, demoralized the country to a very great extent, and it has
only been in the past few years the negro laborers have realized their true
conditions and gone to work with a view of making a support for themselves and families. There is yet much room for improvement, but they
will improve just as they gain experience and become self-reliant.

Considering their condition after emancipation and the evil influences
to which they have been subjected, even the small advancement they have
made seems surprising.

Question 2. Under what systems are the laborers in your section employed?—*Answer.* There are three methods: we hire for wages [or] for
a part of the crop, or we rent.

Question 3. When hired for wages what is paid?—*Answer.* When hired
by the month we pay unskilled field-hands from $10 to $20 per month and
board. When hired by the day, for unskilled laborers, from 75 cents to $1.
Teamsters, $1 a day and board. Artisans, from $2 to $5. In addition to
their wages and board, the laborers are furnished, free of cost, a house,
fuel, and a garden spot varying from ½ to 1 acre; also the use of wagon
and team with which to haul their fuel and supplies, and pasturage, where
they have cattle and hogs, which they are encouraged to raise.

Question 4. What division is made between labor and capital of their
joint production when you work on shares?—*Answer.* I doubt if there is
greater liberality shown to laborers in any portion of the world than is

done under this system. The proprietor furnishes the land and houses, including dwelling, stables, and out-houses, pays the taxes, makes all necessary improvements, keeps up repairs and insurance, gives free of cost a garden spot, fuel, pasturage for the stock owned by the laborers, and allows the use of his teams for hauling fuel and family supplies, provides mules or horses, wagons, gears, implements, feed for teams, the necessary machinery for ginning, or, in short, every expense of making the crop and preparing it for market, and then divides equally the whole gross proceeds with the laborers. . . . Under this system thrifty, industrious laborers ought soon to become land-owners. But, owing to indolence, the negroes, except where they are very judiciously managed and encouraged, fail to take advantage of the opportunities offered them to raise the necessaries of life. They idle away all the time not actually necessary to make and gather their corn and cotton, and improvidently spend what balance may remain after paying for the advances made to them.

Question 5. When you rent, what division is made?—*Answer.* Where the laborer owns his own teams, gears, and implements necessary for making a crop, he gets two-thirds or three-fourths of the crop, according to the quality and location of the land.

Under the rental system proper, where a laborer is responsible and owns his team, &c., first-class land is rented to him for $8 or $10 per acre. With the land go certain privileges, such as those heretofore enumerated.

Question 6. How many hours do the laborers work?—Answer. This is an extremely difficult question to answer. Under the wages system, from sunrise to sunset, with a rest for dinner of from one and one-half to three hours, according to the season of the year.

Under the share or rental system there is much time lost; for instance, they seldom work on Saturday at all, and as the land is fertile, and a living can be made on a much smaller acreage than a hand can cultivate, they generally choose one-third less than they should, and it is safe to say that one-third of the time which could and would be utilized by an industrious laborer is wasted in fishing, hunting, and idleness.

Question 7. Under what system do you work?—*Answer.* We are forced to adopt all of the systems heretofore stated. We prefer, however, the tenant system. We wish to make small farmers of our laborers, and bring them up as nearly as possible to the standard of the small white farmers. But this can only be done gradually, because the larger portion of the negroes are without any personal property. We could not afford to sell mules, implements, &c., where a laborer has nothing. Therefore the first year we contract to work with him on the half-share system, and require him to plant a portion of the land he cultivates in corn, hay, potatoes, &c. For this portion we charge him a reasonable rent, to be paid out of his part of the cotton raised on the remainder. In this way all of the supplies raised belong to him, and at the end of the first year he will, if industrious, find himself possessed of enough supplies to support and feed a mule. We then sell him a mule and implements, preserving, of course, liens until paid. At the end of the second year, if he should be unfortunate, and not quite pay out, we carry the balance over to the next year, and in this way we gradually make a tenant of him. . . . Under whatever system we work, we require the laborer to plant a part of his land in food crops and the balance in cotton with which to pay his rent and give him ready money. . . . We recognize that no country can be prosperous unless the farmers are prosperous. Under our system, we seek to have our property cultivated by a reliable set of tenants, who will be able to always pay their rent and have a surplus left.

Again, a large portion of the cotton crop in the country is made by small white farmers. These to a great extent are raising their own supplies, and making cotton a surplus crop. The number who do this will increase year by year. It must be apparent that the large planters cannot afford to hire labor and compete with those whose cotton costs nothing except the expenditure of their own muscle and energy. The natural consequence resulting from this condition of things is that the negro, if he is to prosper, must gradually become a small farmer, either as a tenant or the owner of the soil, and look himself upon cotton as a surplus crop.

Question 8. What is the relation existing between the planters and their employés?—*Answer.* Friendly and harmonious. The planter feels an interest in the welfare of his laborers, and the latter in turn look to him for advice and assistance.

Question 9. What danger is there of strikes?—*Answer.* Very little. As a rule the laborers are interested in the production of the soil, and a strike would be as disastrous to them as it would be to the proprietors. There is really very little conflict between labor and capital. The conflict in my section, if any should come in the future, will not assume the form of labor against capital, but of race against race.

Question 10. How can the interest of the laborers of your section be best subserved?—*Answer.* By the establishment by the States of industrial schools, by the total elimination from Federal politics of the so-called negro question, and by leaving its solution to time, and a reduction of taxation, both indirect and incidental. It is a noteworthy fact that the improvement of my section has kept pace, *pari passu,* with the cessation of the agitation of race issues. The laborers share equally with the land owners the advantages of the improvement, and there is every reason to expect increasing and permanent prosperity if all questions between the land owners and their laborers in our section are left to the natural adjustment of the demand for labor. For many years the negroes regarded themselves as the wards of the Federal Government, and it were well for them to understand that they have nothing more to expect from the Federal Government than the white man, and that, like him, their future depends upon their own energy, industry, and economy. This can work no hardship. The constant demand for their labor affords them the amplest protection. Nothing, probably, would contribute so immediately to their prosperity as the reduction of the tariff. They are the producers of no protected articles. The onerous burdens of the tariff naturally fall heaviest upon those who are large consumers of protected articles and produce only the great staples, grain and cotton, which form the basis of our export trade, and which can, from their very nature in this country, receive no protection from a tariff.

[20.] *"The Black Farmers ... Are Robbed"*

A prominent Negro (T. Thomas Fortune, editor of the *New York Globe*) replies to the testimony of John C. Calhoun. [Senate Committee on Education and Labor, *The Relations Between Labor and Capital* . . . (Washington, D. C.: United States Government Printing Office, 1885), II, 526-27.]

. . . I am free to admit that a large percentum of the negroes squander much time and money in fishing, hunting and loafing; still the great mass of the people are honest, steady laborers. They must of necessity be, else how account for the steady increase of production in the South?

Compensation of Farm Laborers in Southern States

Now, in view of these facts, it will naturally be asked why the negro population continues poor and ignorant. The answer, in part, is a direct refutation of the statement made to your honorable committee on Thursday last by Mr. John C. Calhoun as to the rate of wages and how it is paid in the South. The average rate of wages of a farm laborer in the South is nearer fifty than seventy-five cents, out of which the laborer must feed and clothe his family. He seldom ever pays rent and he eldom ever sees a cent of currency. He is paid in "orders" on some store-keeper friendly to the planter. He cannot negotiate these precious "orders" at any other than the store indicated. Hence a system of fraud is connived at and practiced, to the utter demoralization and impoverishment of the ignorant, helpless laborer.

I remember an instance which strikingly illustrates the pernicious features of the "orders" system. At a place on the Suwannee River in Florida there is a large saw-mill, owned by a gentleman who also operates a large farm. This man owns the entire village and all the land for miles around, and he will not allow any one to sell on his land. He owns the only store within forty miles of his place. He pays his employés in "orders" on his store, white and black alike, and it is a rare occasion indeed when any one of them gets his hand on a real dollar bill. So expensive is it to live at this place because of the miserly monopoly of everything by the proprietor, that I have known men who had fallen out with the proprietor to walk away, having been unable, from the earnings of many months, to save sufficient to indulge the luxury of a railroad ticket. I once attended a panoramic exhibition in the little church at this place, when the book-keeper of the firm, a very fine gentleman, stood at the door and "passed in" all his employés who desired to see the sights, noting the name of each in his little book. When they had all passed in he gave the showman an "order" for his money and told him to call at the office the following day and collect, which was done. This sort of thing breeds improvidence, but not thriftlessness, because to be improvident the "orders" must be obtainable, and they are only obtainable when the work has been performed.

Share-Labor System on Farms

The system of share labor is equally unsatisfactory to the laborer. He is compelled to give a lien on his unplanted or unharvested crop to be able to run his farm, and his account at the store at the end of the year usually brings him in debt. My father once kept an account in the liberal sense; that is to say, he kept an account of the things he "took up" at the store as well as the storekeeper. When the accounts were footed up at the end of the year the thing became serious. The storekeeper had one hundred and fifty dollars more against my father than appeared on the latter's book. Of course there was a wide difference of opinion, but my father settled the account according to his book and told the merchant he was at liberty to sue for the remainder. But the merchant failed to do it, and his books will show a shortage of $150 to-day if he has not balanced the account to profit and loss. But of course the mass of colored men who farm on shares or labor by the year and keep an account do not, because they cannot, keep a record of every purchase; and it is by this means that they are swindled and kept forever in debt.

I have known honest but ignorant colored men who have lost large farms, magnificently accoutered, by such thievery. The black farmers, and those in other occupations at the South, are robbed year after year by the simplest sort of devices; and the very men who rob them are the loudest in complaint that the negroes are lazy and improvident. For my part, I am surprised that a larger number of them do not go to fishing, hunting and loafing.

[21.] *"The Increase in the Large Farms ...*
Has Been 800 Per Cent"

William Godwin Moody, champion of labor and the small independent farmer, describes the advantages enjoyed by the bonanza farmer. [Senate Committee on Education and Labor, *The Relations Between Labor and Capital* . . . (Washington, D. C.: United States Government Printing Office, 1885), I, 732-35, 977-79.]

. . . This whole question of the farming interest is a very important one, and to show you another of the evils that grow out of these railroad grants and that are incident to them, I will refer to the fact that there is a very rapid change of ownership being made in the farming lands; that the small farmer as the owner of his farm is rapidly disappearing. Our whole northern country is filled with loan agents. In every considerable town and city you find often where they make a sole business of lending money upon farm lands and taking mortgages, and a large proportion of that money so loaned is foreign capital—a very large proportion.

Now this is true of the old farms in the old settled parts of the country as well as of the new, and it is a common subject of remark, or used to be a few years ago, the decadence of the farming interest in the Northern and Middle States.

•   •   •

Question. . . . I understood you to say that an industrious, economical, prudent farmer upon the average soil of the Middle, Northern, and Northwestern States is not able to obtain a comfortable support, the comforts, or even the necessaries of life, from the productions of his farm resulting from his own labor; that the owner of land working it in that way cannot procure from it a comfortable subsistence for himself and his family. Do you mean to say that?—*Answer.* Yes, sir; under present conditions. That means (to make myself thoroughly understood) at the prices which he receives for his products, and with the competition that he is now compelled to contend against. I do say that under such conditions he cannot get a comfortable and assured subsistence for himself and his family.

By the CHAIRMAN:

Question. You are referring now to the small farmer, the homesteader, not to the large farmers who work these factory farms?—*Answer.* I mean the small farmer. The large farmer, on the other hand, finds his investment one of the very best investments known to capital at the present day. The land commissioner of the Saint Paul and Sioux City Railroad said to me in 1879, and he gave me a circular making the same claim, that the man who went there and bought a very considerable tract of land and put it in wheat, would pay for his whole investment, land, wheat, and all the first year, and make a very considerable percentage beyond, and that after the first year it would pay him for his investment at a rate not less than 50 per cent.

Advantages of Wholesale Farming

By Mr. CALL:

Question. Now give us the reason why that is so; why the big farmer makes money at that rate while the small farmer, who works himself, loses no time, sees that all the economies are properly observed, and farms with equal or greater skill, fails to make money, or even to make a comfortable living, according to your statement.—*Answer.* I thank you for the question. That is just the question I want to answer.

• • •

. . . The large farmer employs his labor only during the time when that labor can be profitably employed in the production of the crop, he pays wages that but very little more than furnish an absolute subsistence to his laborers during the time that they are actually employed. When the necessity for their employment has terminated all expenses on that score have stopped except what may be necessary for the care of his cattle. The laborers, the human cattle employed upon his farm, are sent adrift. They may go and fish or grub for themselves as best they can, while the brute animals are taken care of by two or three men, or perhaps only one.

Therefore you see the labor, and consequently the necessity of supplying subsistence to that labor, upon such a farm has been reduced to the absolute minimum; indeed you may call it *nil.*

By Mr. GEORGE:

Question. What is the price of agricultural labor here? Is not the laborer fed and lodged?—*Answer.* He is fed and lodged.

Question. Beyond that what wages does he get?—*Answer.* It runs from $6 to $15 a month.

By the CHAIRMAN:

Question. Are you referring now to the agricultural labor of the East or of the West, or of any particular part of the country?—*Answer.* I am speaking of the wages paid to agricultural laborers in the great grain-growing sections generally, except during the harvest season. During that season—which will extend over ten, fifteen, or twenty days, or perhaps a little longer—the men will get wages of about $1 to $1.50 a day. I have spoken of the economies of the great farmer; let us turn now to the small farmer.

By Mr. CALL:

Question. You say that the great farmer does not employ his laborers when he does not need them.—*Answer.* That is it exactly.

•   •   •

Disadvantages of the Small Farmer

Answer. There is one part of Senator Call's question which I have not answered, in regard to the economies of the small farmer. In the first place, such a farmer has more than his individual self to support. He has in all probability a wife. A good wife is never a drawback to a farmer, nor do I wish to be understood as implying that she is; but still the small farmer has a wife who must be fed and clothed; he has children who must be fed and clothed, and nursed, and educated, and cared for in every sense. Now these burdens of the small farmer—

Mr. CALL (*Interposing*). They are not burdens to the farmer; they all become assistants in production.

The WITNESS. Then we will put it in another way. These necessities of the farmer's family do not terminate with the termination of the work that is done in the production of the crop as do the necessities of the large farmer for feeding the laborer employed on his bonanza farm. The demands upon the small farmer for food and clothing, and all the other necessaries of life, for a considerable number of persons, continue the year through and must be supplied for the full year from the products of his own labor. It is not so with the large farmer. With him the demands upon the production of his farm last only for the few weeks that the productive labor lasts; but in the other case the demands last for the whole twelve months.

• • •

In further answer to your question, Mr. Chairman, I will say that beyond the facts I have already stated, beyond the difference in the time occupied and in the expense chargeable against the product in the two cases, the large farmer has all the advantages of the use of the steam-plow, the steam-thrasher, harvesters, cultivators, rollers, and all the machinery that is in use upon those large farms, and which cannot be brought into use by the small farmer, even by co-operation, or at least cannot be brought into use nearly so economically as they can be by the large farmer, where the whole of the work is upon his own farm.

• • •

Question. You are going on now to show us what will be the condition of things when these improvements are in general use, are you not?— *Answer.* I have been telling you what is the fact at the present time. Now, with regard to the small farmer being able to use the steam-thrasher, it is obvious that the thrasher would have to be changed every two or three days, or perhaps oftener, from one farm to another, so that the necessity for these changes would make it impossible for the small farmer to use the machine economically. That applies to grain, and the same is true in regard to corn. In the large corn fields they will put in two, three, four, or even ten horse huskers, and husk thousands of bushels of corn in a day. Those machines remain in the field at points convenient for use, being but rarely moved, and they will shell vast quantities of corn at a very slight expense. But they cannot be used successfully by the small farmer, for the same reason that applies to the grain machinery. Therefore, the small farmer is compelled to make use of the less powerful and less economical machines. So that in every point of view the small farmer is at a disadvantage as compared with the large farmer.

Increase in the Number of Large Farms

I think I heard you [Mr. Call] say just now that large farms do not prevail to any great extent in this country. Let me give you some figures on that subject. . . .

• • •

. . . Whereas in 1870 the total number of small farms was about 3,000,-000, there were in 1880 about 4,000,000, which shows an increase during that decade of about 33 per cent. In the same decade the increase in the large farms of 1,000 acres and over has been 800 per cent.

Evils of the Bonanza Farm System

Question. Therefore, you consider that in the future there are to be more and more of the large farms?—*Answer.* That is the way I look at it.

Question. And prospectively you see evils resulting?—*Answer.* I not only see evils prospectively, but I find evils existing at the present time. I find vast tracts of our country without an inhabitant; I find the people absolutely debarred from access to vast tracts of our territory, and at the same time I find our cities crowded with population, a large portion of whom are in the condition of paupers. Your committee has seen something of that in the city of New York. Every city in the Union and every considerable town has more or less of the horrors which you have witnessed in the tenement-houses here.

Question. And your theory I understand to be that all those horrors are endured and have to be endured because people cannot make a comfortable subsistence from agricultural labor?—*Answer.* What I mean to say is that all these horrors have grown up coincidently with these great holdings, these vast monopolies of every name and nature, that I have described. Now, it is for this committee, in common with the whole world, to decide whether there is any connection between these two sets of facts. I am simply giving the facts.

[22.] *"There Is Something Wrong in All This"*

S. M. Smith, Secretary of the Illinois State Farmers' Association, talks freely with a *New York Tribune* reporter. [Edward Winslow Martin (pseudonym for James Dabney McCabe), *History of the Grange Movement* . . . (Philadelphia: National Publishing Company, 1873), pp. 364-65.]

I can give you some striking examples of the profit of raising corn and wheat in this vicinity, if you desire. One forenoon a man went past here with a load of sixty bushels of corn. He said that he had come a long distance—had started at four o'clock in the morning. As he returned in the afternoon, I asked him how much he had got for his load of corn. He held up two pairs of boys' boots, and said that his sixty bushels of corn, and $1 in cash, had just purchased them. It took at least seven days' labor of a man and team to raise that corn, and another long day to haul it to market, to say nothing of interest on the farmer's investment and other expenses. I judge that each pair of boots cost about five days' labor, or its equivalent. I knew another man who took a ton of corn to market for the purpose of buying coal. It purchased just a ton, and he spent a day with his team in hauling. One year I raised 3600 bushels of wheat, and kept a careful account of its cost. When I sold it, and balanced my books, I found that I had for my own labor, which I had not charged, and that of my wife, who had a terribly hard time of it cooking for harvesters and threshers during the hot weather of midsummer, just $300! Why, sir, $1000 would not have paid for that summer's work. Wheat is so uncertain a crop, it has so many enemies from the time it is sown until it is threshed, and it is so exacting of the farmer who must attend to it at certain time, or he will lose it, that we can't afford to raise it for less than ninety cents a bushel.

Now there is something wrong in all this. With our productive soil, and facilities for reaching market, the farmers of Illinois ought to be forehanded, comfortably housed and clothed, and able to save a little every year, instead of getting deeper and deeper into debt. We are an intelligent, hard-working, economical people, and every one of us who owns his farm is to that extent a capitalist; and we ought to be able to do as well as the journeyman mechanic, with less education than we and no capital. It is not right that the Chicago, Burlington & Quincy Railroad, which only moves our crop to Chicago, a distance of 132 miles, and the trade in that city who handles it, should be growing enormously rich, while we are growing poorer. It is not worth eleven cents a bushel to take our corn from here to Chicago, and the railroad that is charging it is robbing us of a part of the fruits of our labor.

[23.] *"The Gilding of Farm Life Melted Away"*

Hamlin Garland recalls Saturday night with the farmhands and his return a few years later to the scenes of his boyhood. [Hamlin Garland, *A Son of the Middle Border* (New York: The Macmillan Company, 1917), pp. 175-77, 358, 361-65. © 1917 by Hamlin Garland, renewed 1945 by Mary I. Lord and Constance G. Williams. Reprinted by permission of The Macmillan Company and The Bodley Head.]

Saturday night in town! How it all comes back to me! I am a timid visitor in the little frontier village. It is sunset. A whiskey-crazed farmhand is walking bare footed up and down the middle of the road defying the world.—From a corner of the street I watch with tense interest another lithe, pock-marked bully menacing with cat-like action, a cowering young farmer in a long linen coat. The crowd jeers at him for his cowardice—a burst of shouting is heard. A trampling follows and forth from the door of a saloon bulges a throng of drunken, steaming, reeling, cursing ruffians followed by brave Jim McCarty, the city marshal, with an offender under each hand.—The scene changes to the middle of the street. I am one of a throng surrounding a smooth-handed faker who is selling prize boxes of soap and giving away dollars.—"Now, gentlemen," he says, "if you will hand me a dollar I will give you a sample package of soap to examine, afterwards if you don't want the soap, return it to me, and I'll return your dollar." He repeats this several times, returning the dollars faithfully, then slightly varies his invitation by saying, "so that I *can* return your dollars."

No one appears to observe this significant change, and as he has hitherto returned the dollars precisely according to promise, he now proceeds to his harvest. Having all his boxes out he abruptly closes the lid of his box and calmly remarks, "I said, 'so that I *can* return your dollars,' I didn't say I would.—Gentlemen, I have the dollars and *you* have the experience." He drops into his seat and takes up the reins to drive away. A tall man who has been standing silently beside the wheel of the carriage, snatches the whip from its socket, and lashes the swindler across the face. Red streaks appear on his cheek.—The crowd surges forward. Up from behind leaps a furious little Scotchman who snatches off his right boot and beats the stranger over the head with such fury that he falls from his carriage to the ground.—I rejoice in his punishment, and admire the tall man who led the assault.—The marshal comes, the man is led away, and the crowd smilingly scatters.—

We are on the way home. Only two of my crew are with me. The others are roaring from one drinking place to another, having a "good time." The air is soothingly clean and sweet after the tumult and the reek of the town. Appalled, yet fascinated, I listen to the oft repeated tales of just how Jim McCarty sprang into the saloon and cleaned out the brawling mob. I feel very young, very defenceless, and very sleepy as I listen.—

      •   •   •

At last the train came, and as it rattled away to the north and I drew closer to the scenes of my boyhood, my memory quickened. The Cedar rippling over its limestone ledges, the gray old mill and the pond where I used to swim, the farm-houses with their weedy lawns, all seemed not only familiar but friendly, and when at last I reached the station (the same grimy little den from which I had started forth six years before), I rose from my seat with the air of a world-traveller and descended upon the warped and splintered platform, among my one time friends and neighbors, with quickened pulse and seeking eye.

      •   •   •

As I walked the street I met several neighbors from Dry Run as well as acquaintances from the Grove. Nearly all, even the young men, looked worn and weather-beaten and some appeared both silent and sad. Laughter was curiously infrequent and I wondered whether in my days on the farm they had all been as rude of dress, as misshapen of form and as wistful of voice as they now seemed to me to be. "Have times changed? Has a spirit of unrest and complaining developed in the American farmer?"

      •   •   •

From the window of a law office, Emma and Matilda Leete were leaning and I decided to make myself known to them. Emma, who had been one of my high admirations, had developed into a handsome and interesting woman with very little of the village in her dress or expression, and when I stepped up to her and asked, "Do you know me?" her calm gray eyes and smiling lips denoted humor. "Of course I know you—in spite of the beard. Come in and sit with us and tell all us about yourself."

As we talked, I found that they, at least, had kept in touch with the thought of the east, and . . . [Emma] understood in some degree the dark mood which I voiced. She, too, occasionally doubted whether the life they were all living was worth while. "We make the best of it," she said, "but none of us are living up to our dreams."

      •   •   •

Returning to the street, I introduced myself to Uncle Billy Fraser and Osmund Button and other Sun Prairie neighbors and when it became known that "Dick Garland's boy" was in town, many friends gathered about to shake my hand and inquire concerning "Belle" and "Dick."

The hard, crooked fingers, which they laid in my palm completed the sorrowful impression which their faces had made upon me. A twinge of pain went through my heart as I looked into their dim eyes and studied their heavy knuckles. I thought of the hand of Edwin Booth, of the flower-like palm of Helena Modjeska, of the subtle touch of Inness, and I said, "Is it not time that the human hand ceased to be primarily a bludgeon for hammering a bare living out of the earth? Nature all bountiful, undiscriminating, would, under justice, make such toil unnecessary." My heart burned with indignation. With William Morris and Henry George I exclaimed, "Nature is not to blame. Man's laws are to blame,"—but of this I said nothing at the time—at least not to men like Babcock and Fraser.

Next day I rode forth among the farms of Dry Run, retracing familiar lanes, standing under the spreading branches of the maple trees I had planted fifteen years before. I entered the low stone cabin wherein Neighbor Button had lived for twenty years (always intending sometime to build a house and make a granary of this), and at the table with the family and the hired men, I ate again of Ann's "riz" biscuit and sweet melon pickles. It was not a pleasant meal, on the contrary it was depressing to me. The days of the border were over, and yet Arvilla his wife was ill and aging, still living in pioneer discomfort toiling like a slave.

At neighbor Gardner's home, I watched his bent complaining old wife housekeeping from dawn to dark, literally dying on her feet. William Knapp's home was somewhat improved but the men still came to the table in their shirt sleeves smelling of sweat and stinking of the stable, just as they used to do, and Mrs. Knapp grown more gouty, more unwieldly than ever (she spent twelve or fourteen hours each day on her swollen and aching feet), moved with a waddling motion because, as she explained, "I can't limp—I'm just as lame in one laig as I am in t'other. But 'tain't no use to complain, I've just so much work to do and I might as well go ahead and do it."

I slept that night in her "best room," yes, at last, after thirty years of pioneer life, she had a guest chamber and a new "bed-room soot." With open pride and joy she led Belle Garland's boy in to view this precious acquisition, pointing out the soap and towels, and carefully removing the counterpane! I understood her pride, for my mother had not yet acquired anything so luxurious as this. She was still on the border!

•   •   •

Every house I visited had its individual message of sordid struggle and half-hidden despair. Agnes had married and moved away to Dakota, and Bess had taken upon her girlish shoulders the burdens of wifehood and motherhood almost before her girlhood had reached its first period of bloom. In addition to the work of being cook and scrub-woman, she was now a mother and nurse. As I looked around upon her worn chairs, faded rag carpets, and sagging sofas,—the bare walls of her pitiful little house seemed a prison. I thought of her as she was in the days of her radiant girlhood and my throat filled with rebellious pain.

All the gilding of farm life melted away. The hard and bitter realities came back upon me in a flood. Nature was as beautiful as ever. The soaring sky was filled with shining clouds, the tinkle of the bobolink's fairy bells rose from the meadow, a mystical sheen was on the odorous grass and waving grain, but no splendor of cloud, no grace of sunset could conceal the poverty of these people, on the contrary they brought out, with a more intolerable poignancy, the gracelessness of these homes, and the sordid quality of the mechanical daily routine of these lives.

· · ·

Men who were growing bent in digging into the soil spoke to me of their desire to see something of the great eastern world before they died. Women whose eyes were faded and dim with tears, listened to me with almost breathless interest whilst I told them of the great cities I had seen, of wonderful buildings, of theaters, of the music of the sea. Young girls expressed to me their longing for a life which was better worth while, and lads, eager for adventure and excitement, confided to me their secret intention to leave the farm at the earliest moment. "I don't intend to wear out my life drudging on this old place," said Wesley Fancher with a bitter oath.

IV

LABOR

None felt the impact of the machine more than the laboring men. It robbed some of them of their jobs while it created new jobs for others. It rendered many skills obsolete, enabling machine tenders to replace craftsmen, but it also required new skills and increased the band of white-collar workers to an army. By substituting the large factory for the small shop, the machine destroyed the close relationship between employer and employee, but the estranged employee enjoyed better working conditions, shorter hours, and higher pay in the impersonal factory. The machine deprived many workers of their tools, skills, and bargaining power, but by bringing together men with similar interests made labor unions inevitable.

Unskilled labor, however, did not organize effectively during the Gilded Age, nor did craft unions of skilled workers match the strength of organized capital. Though small strikes were occasionally successful, major showdowns between capital and labor ended disastrously for labor. Unions were destroyed, labor leaders were fired and "black-listed," laborers returned to work on management's terms signing "yellow-dog contracts" certifying that they would not rejoin a union. The corporation was more than a match for labor, and when backed by public opinion and governmental action proved invincible. Considered by many to be contrary to the American ideal of individualism, unions and strikes were publicly condemned and blamed for violence and labor unrest. Whether skilled or unskilled, organized or unorganized, unions did benefit most Gilded Age laborers. Modest goals were achieved. The shorter hours, better working conditions, and higher pay achieved by skilled, organized labor frequently led to improvements for unskilled, unorganized labor.

[24.] *"The Pay . . . Is Good, But the Labor Is Hard"*

A French economist assesses the impact of the machine on American labor. [E. Levasseur, "The Concentration of Industry, and Machinery in the United States," *Annals of the American Academy of Political and Social Science,* Vol. IX, No. 2 (March 1897), 12-14, 18-19, 21-24.]

"The pay here is good, but the labor is hard," said an Alsatian blacksmith employed in a large factory. I could verify nearly everywhere the truth of this remark, for I have seen such activity both in the small industry, where the tailors in the sweating-shops in New York worked with feverish rapidity, and in the great industry, where the butchers of the Armour packing house prepared 5800 hogs a day, where the cotton weavers tended as many as eight looms, or where the rolling-mill in Chicago turned out 1000 tons of rails in a day. Everywhere the machine goes very rapidly, and it commands; the workman has to follow. An English manufacturer, having read in one of Mr. [Jacob] Schoenhof's books that a silk spinner of New Jersey had renewed his machinery in order to obtain 7500 turns a minute, instead of 5000, told him that should he establish such machinery in his workshop all his workers would leave him. And, yet, in America, at the present time, the rapidity is from 10,000 to 13,000 turns.

Even where the machine only plays a secondary rôle it is customary to go quickly and to lose no time, a necessary result of competition. The employer will not tolerate an idle or listless laborer, who causes him loss.

In the Senate inquiry of 1883, upon education and labor, a weaver of Fall River, who had been a member of the Massachusetts Legislature, and who was then secretary of the Weavers' Union, said that he had worked seventeen years in England, and that conditions were much better than in America. The manufacturers there were not so desirous as they are here of working their men like horses or slaves; they do not work with the extraordinary rapidity which is customary at Fall River. In England, one man manages a pair of looms with two assistants; one between the looms and the other behind. In America, the manufacturer, with one or two exceptions, will not hear of that, and whatever the number of spindles they do not wish that a man shall have more than one assistant. The spindle is turned more rapidly; the laborers have more to do and for each loom Fall River produces more.

In the same investigation, a tailor who had been successively miner, farm hand, and tailor in England, and who was secretary of a union at New York, thought the miner better off in England than he was in America, where he was obliged to do much more work in a day. "One can," he said, "say the same of carpenters, bricklayers, and plasterers. For instance, a bricklayer sets in a day about 500 bricks more than at London, Liverpool or Glasgow. I have lived in these cities and I have studied the question. A bricklayer here does more and better than elsewhere. The same is true of the carpenter and the cabinetmaker. In all the branches of industry, the men have to labor harder than in England, and their day is longer." The last statement would no longer be exact in 1893.

The superintendent for a large contractor and builder at St. Cloud, Minn., replied in an investigation by the Bureau of Labor, that workmen in the building trades who had served an apprenticeship in Europe, were slow in their work, even when they knew it well. On the other hand, a foreman stonecutter stated that the best laborers were those who had learned the trade in Europe, especially in Scotland, because they commenced their apprenticeship later and continued it longer.

Several French laborers, delegates to the Exposition at Chicago, have brought back from their trip the notion that the laborer has to work hard and that he cannot loaf or chatter. "In the machine-shops," said one of them, "there is no movement, no going from place to place on the part of workmen, each one remains at his post without the discipline being more severe than in France."

A Frenchman, a former student of the School of Art and Trades of Aix, who had worked many years as a machinist in America, gave me his experience on this point: "The American workman," he said,

is very conscientious, he does not leave his place to talk with his comrades, he is very active and he knows how to use the machine which he handles with intelligence and not with mere routine. Thus, when he makes the cogwheels, it is not unusual for him to modify the pattern which is before him. In such a case he notifies his foreman, who usually approves it. He enjoys great liberty in regard to the carrying out of his work. If he has invented anything, the employer, as a rule, encourages him [I observed this myself in the box factory connected with the Armour packing house], and oftentimes buys the invention to take out a patent in his own name. Specialty is pushed very far and the same models are frequently used, which facilitates the little inventions of detail, because the attention of the intelligent workman is constantly fixed upon the same object.

•   •   •

The manufacturers judge that the movement [to mechanize] has been advantageous to workmen, as sellers of labor, because the level of salaries has been raised, as consumers of products, because they purchase more with the same sum, and as laborers, because their task has become less onerous, the machine doing nearly everything which requires great strength; the workman, instead of bringing his muscles into play, has become an inspector, using his intelligence. He is told that his specialized labor is degrading because monotonous. Is it more monotonous to overlook with the eye for ten hours several automatic looms, and to attach, from time to time, one thread to another with the finger, than to push for fourteen hours against the breast the arm of a hand-loom, pressing at the same time the pedals with the feet?

In proportion as the machines require more room, the ceilings become higher, the workshops larger, the hygienic conditions better. From a sanitary standpoint, there is no comparison between the large factory to-day and the hut of the peasant, or the tenement of the sweating system. The improvement of machinery and the growing power of industrial establishments, have diminished the price of a great number of goods, and this is one of the most laudable forward movements of industry whose object is to satisfy, as well as possible, the needs of man.

The laboring classes do not share this optimism. They reproach the machine with exhausting the physical powers of the laborer; but this can only apply to a very small number of cases to those where the workman is at the same time the motive power, as in certain sewing-machines. They reproach it with demanding such continued attention that it enervates, and of leaving no respite to the laborer, through the continuity of its movement. This second complaint may be applicable in a much larger number of cases, particularly in the spinning industries and in weaving, where the workman manages more than four looms. They reproach the machine with degrading man by transforming him into a machine, which knows how to make but one movement, and that always the same. They reproach it with diminishing the number of skilled laborers, permitting in many cases the substitution of unskilled workers and lowering the average level of wages. They reproach it with depriving, momentarily at least, every time that an invention modifies the work of the factory, a certain number of workmen of their means of subsistence, thus rendering the condition of all uncertain. They reproach it, finally, with reducing absolutely and permanently the number of persons employed for wages, and thus being indirectly injurious to all wage-earners who make among themselves a more disastrous competition, the more the opportunities for labor are restricted.

In one of the reports of the census of 1880, Mr. [Carroll D.] Wright examined other accusations which have been brought generally against manufacturing: (1) necessitating the employment of an excessive number of women and children, it tends to destroy the family ties; (2) it is injurious to health; (3) it tends toward intemperance, prodigality, and pauperism; (4) it encourages prostitution and criminality. It was not difficult to prove that these accusations rest upon errors or exaggerations.

• • •

To these grievances political economy replies by the general results of statistics, which show that the total number of laborers, far from having diminished, has steadily increased from one census to another in the United States; that, on the other hand, the total wages paid to laborers shows an increase of average wages, that the diminution in the price of goods is advantageous to consumers among whom are to be reckoned the wage-earners. These three facts are indisputable.

However, the American laborer is not reassured by such a reply, because he rarely consumes the goods he manufactures, because the average wages of the country is not necessarily the measure of his wages; because when dismissed in consequence of an improvement of machinery, he runs great risk of finding no employment in the same industry, while in another he finds it generally only after long delays; in the meantime, he has a family to support. Although the American is more mobile than the European, the transition is not easy either for one or the other. And on both sides of the Atlantic, there is individual misery and professional crises which touch painfully, very cruelly sometimes, the laboring classes. That fact is not to be disputed.

• • •

The chief of the Labor Bureau of New York has made a suggestive comparison: the United States and Great Britain, he says, are the countries which own and use the most machines. Compare the general condition of laborers in those countries with that of any country whatever in the world, where machines are unknown, except in the most primitive forms. Where is the superiority? It is almost a paradox, and yet it is a truth that machines bring about a much larger employment and improvement, not only because they increase production, but because they multiply the chances of employment, and incidentally the consumption of products. In fact, the census of the United States shows that the proportion of laborers to the total number of inhabitants has increased in the same period that the machine has taken most complete possession of manufactures. From 1860 to 1890, while the population of the United States doubled, the number of persons employed in industry increased nearly threefold (increase of 172 per cent), and at the same time the mechanical power, measured by horsepower, increased fourfold. Inventions have created new industries, such as photography, electricity, telegraphy, electrotyping, railroading, manufacture of bicycles, etc., and have thus given to labor much more employment than they have withdrawn from it. Thus, even in old industries, transformed by machinery, the progress of consumption has generally maintained a demand for hands.

• • •

There is no social evolution which does not produce friction. That which urges industry toward machinery and large factories appears to me to-day irresistible, because it leads to cheapness, which the consumer seeks first of all, and which is one of the objects of economic civilization. It is Utopia to believe that the world could come back by some modification of the social order, or of mechanical motive powers to the system of the little family workshop. Such a workshop is far from being an ideal, as the sweating system proves.

[25.] *"The Name of the Sweaters Is Legion"*

The State Inspector of Factories and Workshops for Illinois exposes the condition of unorganized labor in a relatively unmechanized industry. [Florence Kelley, "The Sweating-System," in *Hull-House Maps and Papers* . . . (New York: Thomas Y. Crowell & Co., 1895), pp. 27-35, 37-40.]

The sweating-system is confined in Chicago to the garment trades, which employ some 25,000 to 30,000 people (as nearly as we can estimate), among whom this system is found in all its modes and tenses. The manufacture of garments is in the hands of wholesale firms. Their factories are grouped in the first ward of the city, within a radius of four blocks, where they have large, well-lighted, fairly wholesome workrooms, in which the garments for the entire trade are cut. The cutters, having a strong organization, refuse to work except under conditions more or less equal with the conditions of work usual in the well-organized trades. The hours and wages prevailing in the cutters' shops, therefore, do not differ much from the hours and wages usual in the well-organized trades. Some of the wholesale manufacturers have not only the cutters' shops, but also large workrooms, in which all the processes of clothing manufacture are carried on. These latter are known as "inside shops," or garment factories; and in them the employees work under conditions vastly better than are imposed upon the sweaters' victims, though still farther than the cutters below the standard of hours and wages maintained in the well-organized trades.

In the inside shops the sanitary conditions are fairly good; and power is frequently, though by no means uniformly, furnished for running machines. . . . The sweating-system has affected disastrously the condition of the employees in the inside shops, since any demand of the inside hands for increased wages or shorter hours is promptly met by transfer of work from the inside shop to a sweater; and the cutters alone remain secure from this competition.

•   •   •

Every manufacturer keeps a list of the names and addresses of the people to whom he gives out garments to be made up, and is required by law to show this list on demand to the factory and workshop inspectors.

It is the duty of the inspectors to follow up these lists, and examine the surroundings amidst which this work is done; and they report that the conditions in which garments are made that are given out from the inside shops for night work and Sunday work differ not a jot from the tenement-house shops and the sweaters' home finishers' dwellings. Thus, a recent night inspection of work given out from one of the largest cloak manufactories in the West resulted as follows: The garment maker was found in his tenement dwelling in the rear of a factory. With his family, a wife and four indescribably filthy children, he occupies a kitchen and two bedrooms. The farther bedroom could be entered only by passing through the other rooms. This farther bedroom, where the man was found at work, was 7 × 7 × 8 feet, and contained a bed, a machine, one chair, a reeking lamp, and two men. The bed seemed not to have been made up in weeks; and in the bed, in a heap, there lay two overcoats, two hats, a mass of bed-covers, and nine fine tan-color capes trimmed with ecru lace, a tenth cape being on the machine in process of stitching. The whole dwelling was found to be crawling with vermin, and the capes were not free from it.

•   •   •

The Sweaters

The name of the sweaters is legion. More than a thousand of their shops have been inspected, and more than eight hundred licensed by the city; while it is an open secret that these numbers fall far below the total actually existing. It is well-nigh impossible to keep perfect lists of sweaters;

since a man may be an operator to-day, a sweater on a small scale next week, may move his shop in the night to avoid the payment of rent, and may be found working as operator in an inside shop at the close of the season.

The sweaters differ from the cutters in their relation to the manufacturers, in that the sweaters have no organization, and are incapable of making any organized demand for a standard of prices. They are separated by differences of religion, nationality, language, and location. As individuals they haggle with the manufacturers, undercutting each other, and calculating upon their power to reduce the pay of their employees below any point to which the manufacturers may reduce theirs; and as individuals they tyrannize over the victims who have the misfortune to work in their shops. There has never been, and there is not now, in Chicago any association of sweaters of any kind whatsoever. There is, therefore, no standard price for the making of any garment, either for the sweater or his victim. With every change of style, there is a change of price, and the tendency of the change is always downward. . . . The consequence of the concentration of the manufacture of garments into short, recurrent seasons is an extreme pressure upon the contractor for the speediest possible return of the garments given him; and, hitherto, this pressure has forced the sweaters' victims to work far into the night, and to disregard Sunday and all holidays. It is the belief of the sweaters' victims as well as of the inspectors, that a rigid enforcement of the eight-hour law within these shops will compel the sweaters to increase the number of employees, enlarge their shops, and so create groups numerically too strong to submit to conditions easily imposed upon ten or a dozen very poor people.

By persistent prosecutions of sweaters found employing children under the age of fourteen years, the practice has been to some extent broken up. During the effort to remove them from these shops, there were found boys whose backs have been made crooked for life by continuous work at heavy machines, and boys and girls unable to speak English, and equally unable to read or write in any language.

The sweaters are found in all parts of the city. They are of nine nationalities, speak nine different languages, and are of several religions. The employees ordinarily follow the nationality and religion of the sweater; though Swedes are sometimes found employing Bohemian children, and Russian Jews are found with employees of various nationalities. In general, however, the language of the shop is the language of the sweater, and follows the nationality of the colony in which it is located.

•   •   •

The shops are, without exception, in tenement houses or in the rear of tenement houses, in two-story buildings facing alleys that are usually unpaved and always noxious with the garbage and refuse of a tenement-house district. If the sweater's shop is in a tenement house, it is sometimes—but very rarely—in the ground floor front room, built for a store and lighted by large store windows. But far more commonly it is a basement, or an attic, or the flat over a saloon, or the shed over a stable. All the tenement houses selected either for shops or home finishers are of the worst and most crowded description. The staircases are narrow, and are used in common by tenants and garment workers, so that infectious diseases breaking out among the swarming children can scarcely fail to be communicated to garments anywhere under the same roof, because the utmost laxity prevails in the matter of isolation. The unsanitary condition of many of these tenement houses, and the ignorance and abject poverty of the tenants, insure the maximum probability of disease; and diphtheria, scarlet-fever, smallpox, typhoid, scabies, and worse forms of skin diseases, have been found in alarming proximity to garments of excellent quality in process of manufacture for leading firms.

There is not in the whole [nineteenth] ward a clothing-shop in any building erected for the purpose; and in no case is steam-power supplied, but the use of foot-power is universal. . . .

•   •   •

Meanwhile, every tenement-house shop is ruinous to the health of the employees. . . .

•   •   •

A typical example is the experience of a cloakmaker who began work at his machine in this ward at the age of fourteen years, and was found, after twenty years of temperate life and faithful work, living in a rear basement, with four of his children apparently dying of pneumonia, at the close of a winter during which they had had, for weeks together, no food but bread and water, and had been four days without bread. The visiting nurse had two of the children removed to a hospital, and nursed the other two safely through their illness, feeding the entire family nearly four months. Place after place was found for the father; but he was too feeble to be of value to any sweater, and was constantly told that he was not worth the room he took up. A place being found for him in charge of an elevator, he could not stand; and two competent physicians, after a careful examination, agreed that he was suffering from old age. Twenty years at a machine had made him an old man at thirty-four. During these twenty years his earnings had ranged from $260 to $300 per annum.

•   •   •

It is preposterous, on the face of it, that a trade employing from 25,000 to 30,000 persons in a single city, with an annual output of many millions of dollars, should be carried on with the same primitive machines which were used thirty years ago. In every other branch of manufacture the watchword of the present generation has been concentration. Everywhere steam, electricity, and human ingenuity have been pressed into service for the purpose of organization and centralization; but in the garment trades this process has been reversed, and the division of labor has been made a means of demoralization, disorganization, and degradation, carried to a point beyond which it is impossible to go. While the textile mills in which the material for garments is spun and woven have been constantly enlarged and improved, both as to the machinery used and as to the healthfulness of the surroundings of the work-people, the garment trade has been enriched merely by the addition of the buttonhole machine; and this lone, lorn improvement has been made the means of deforming the illiterate children employed at it.

. . . The garment worker . . . still works in his kitchen, perhaps with the aid of his wife, performing one of the dozen subdivisions of the labor of making garments. He rarely belongs to an organization, and if he does it is so weak as to be almost useless to him either for education or defence. If he is an "all-round garment worker," whatever his skill may be, he has little use for it; since, in competition with him, the cutter cuts, the operator stitches, the seam-binder binds seams, the hand-girl fells, the presser presses, the buttonholer makes buttonholes by the thousand gross. Whatever the disadvantages of the division of labor, the garment worker suffers them all. Of its advantages he has never had a taste.

•   •   •

A millionnaire philanthropist, at the head of one of the largest clothing-houses in the world, was once asked why he did not employ directly the people who made his goods, and furnish them with steam-power, thus saving a heavy drain upon their health, and reducing the number of sweaters' victims found every winter in his pet hospital. "So far," he replied, "we have found leg-power and the sweater cheaper."

[26.] *"As a Rule We Do Not Employ a Child Under Ten"*

Hamilton H. Hickman, president of the Graniteville Manufacturing Company in South Carolina, answers questions about
child labor. [Senate Committee on Education and Labor, *The
Relations Between Labor and Capital* . . . (Washington,
D. C.: United States Government Printing Office, 1885), IV,
737.]

Question. What number of operatives do you employ?—*Answer.* About
seven hundred and sixty.

Question. Are they males or females; and, if both, in what proportions?
—*Answer.* We work both male and female operatives, and I suppose that
nearly two-thirds of them are females.

Question. What is the youngest age at which you employ operatives?—
Answer. As a rule we do not employ a child under ten years.

Question. How many have you employed between the ages of ten and
fifteen years?—*Answer.* I suppose probably one hundred and fifty.

Question. What proportion of the one hundred and fifty are under thirteen years of age?—*Answer.* I don't suppose there are over fifty.

Question. You work eleven hours a day, I suppose?—*Answer.* Yes, sir.

Question. What kind of goods do you make?—*Answer.* Shirtings, sheet-
ings, and drillings.

Question. You use No. 14 yarn, I suppose?—*Answer.* Yes, sir. At our
new mill we spin some No. 16 and 18 in making the higher class of goods.

Question. What wages do you pay your weavers?—*Answer.* I don't
know that I can answer that question with as much accuracy as Mr. Cog-
gin could, he being the superintendent. I am the president of the corporation, but I am not a manufacturer. I think, however, that our wages would
average from 80 to 85 cents.

•   •   •

Question. Are the children of the operatives employed in the factories?
—*Answer.* Yes, sir. Every fall, especially when there have been poor crops,
we have a number of country people who have been broken up on their
farms and who come into Graniteville with their families to put them in
the mill, and in many cases the children have to support the parents. Some
of those people, of course, are old and in bad health, and they come there

and locate and the children often support the family. A great many of those are very good people.

[27.] *"It Matters Not That They Are Well-Meaning Capitalists"*

Richard T. Ely, a professor at the University of Wisconsin and a founder of the American Economic Association, describes the company town of Pullman. [Richard T. Ely, "Pullman: A Social Study," *Harper's New Monthly Magazine,* LXX, No. 417 (February 1885), 452-53, 456-57, 460-61, 463-66.]

. . . Several employers have attempted more far-reaching establishments which should embrace the home life of laborers, and thus include wives and children in their beneficence. . . . But the most extensive experiment of this character is that now in progress at Pullman, Illinois. It is social experimentation on a vast scale, and this is its significance.

• • •

Pullman, a town of eight thousand inhabitants, some ten miles from Chicago, on the Illinois Central Railroad, was founded less than four years ago by the Pullman Palace Car Company, whose president and leading spirit is Mr. George M. Pullman. Its purpose was to provide both a centre of industry and homes for the employés of the company and such additional laborers as might be attracted to the place by other opportunities to labor. . . .

• • •

Very gratifying is the impression of the visitor who passes hurriedly through Pullman and observes only the splendid provision for the present material comforts of its residents. What is seen in a walk or drive through the streets is so pleasing to the eye that a woman's first exclamation is certain to be, "Perfectly lovely!" It is indeed a sight as rare as it is delightful. What might have been taken for a wealthy suburban town is given up to busy workers, who literally earn their bread in the sweat of their brow. No favorable sites are set apart for drones living on past accumulations, and if a few short stretches are reserved for residences which can be rented only by those whose earnings are large, this is an exception; and it is not necessary to remain long in the place to notice that clergymen, officers of the company, and mechanics live in adjoining dwellings.

. . .

The Pullman companies retain everything. No private individual owns to-day a square rod of ground or a single structure in the entire town. No organization, not even a church, can occupy any other than rented quarters. With the exception of the management of the public school, every municipal act is here the act of a private corporation. What this means will be perceived when it is remembered that it includes such matters as the location, repairs, and cleaning of streets and sidewalks, the maintenance of the fire department, and the taking of the local census whenever desired. When the writer was in Pullman a census was taken. A superior officer of the company said to an inferior, "I want a census," and told what kind of a census was desired. That was the whole matter. The people of the place had no more to say about it than a resident of Kamtchatka. . . .

. . .

It should be constantly borne in mind that all investments and outlays in Pullman are intended to yield financial returns satisfactory from a purely business point of view. The minimum return expected is six per centum on expenditure, and the town appears to have yielded a far higher percentage on cost up to the present time. Much of the land was bought at less than $200 per acre, and it is likely that the average price paid did not exceed that. A large part of this now yields rent on a valuation of $5000 per acre, and certain sections in the heart of Pullman are to-day more valuable, and will continue to increase in value in the future, if the town grows as is expected. The extreme reluctance of the officers of the company to make precise statements of any kind renders it impossible to obtain the accurate information desired. Yet there seems to be no reason to doubt the emphatic assertion that the whole establishment pays handsomely. . . .

It pays also in another way. The wholesome, cheerful surroundings enable the men to work more constantly and more efficiently. The healthy condition of the residents is a matter of general comment. The number of deaths has been about seven in a thousand per annum, whereas it has been about fifteen in a thousand in the rest of Hyde Park.

It is maintained that Pullman is truly a philanthropic undertaking, although it is intended that it should be a profitable investment, and this is the argument used: If it can be shown that it does pay to provide beautiful homes for laborers, accompanied with all the conditions requisite for wholesome living both for the body and the mind, the example set by Mr. Pullman will find wide imitation. . . .

. . .

But admirable as are the peculiarities of Pullman which have been described, certain unpleasant features of social life in that place are soon noticed by the careful observer, which moderate the enthusiasm one is at first inclined to feel upon an inspection of the external, plainly visible facts, and the picture must be completed before judgment can be pronounced upon it.

•　　•　　•

. . . Nobody regards Pullman as a real home, and, in fact, it can scarcely be said that there are more than temporary residents at Pullman. One woman told the writer she had been in Pullman two years, and that there were only three families among her acquaintances who were there when she came. Her reply to the question, "It is like living in a great hotel, is it not?" was, "We call it camping out." The nature of the leases aggravates this evil. As already stated, all the property in Pullman is owned by the Pullman associations, and every tenant holds his house on a lease which may be terminated on ten days' notice. . . . Furthermore, three-fourths of the laborers in Pullman are employed by the Palace Car Company, and many of those who do not work for it are employed in establishments in which the company as such or a prominent member of it is interested. The power of Bismarck in Germany is utterly insignificant when compared with the power of the ruling authority of the Pullman Palace Car Company in Pullman. Whether the power be exercised rightfully or wrongfully, it is there all the same, and every man, woman, and child in the town is completely at its mercy, and it can be avoided only by emigration. It is impossible within the realm of Pullman to escape from the overshadowing influence of the company, and every resident feels this, and "monopoly" is a word which constantly falls on the ear of the visitor. Large as the place is, it supports no newspaper, through which complaints might find utterance, and one whose official position in the town qualified him to speak with knowledge declared positively that no publication would be allowed which was not under the direct influence of the Pullman Company. A Baptist clergyman, who had built up quite a congregation, once ventured to espouse the cause of a poor family ejected from their house, and gave rather public expression to his feelings. Shortly after his support began to fall away, one member after another leaving, and it has since never been possible to sustain a Baptist organization in Pullman. It is indeed a sad spectacle. Here is a population of eight thousand souls where not one single resident dare speak out openly his opinion about the town in which he lives. One feels that one is mingling with a dependent, servile people. There is an abundance of grievances, but if there lives in Pullman

one man who would give expression to them in print over his own name,
diligent inquiry continued for ten days was not sufficient to find him.

*   *   *

In looking over all the facts of the case the conclusion is unavoidable
that the idea of Pullman is un-American. It is a nearer approach than anything the writer has seen to what appears to be the ideal of the great
German Chancellor. It is not the American ideal. It is benevolent, well-
wishing feudalism, which desires the happiness of the people, but in such
way as shall please the authorities. . . .

*   *   *

. . . Not a few have ventured to express the hope that Pullman might
be widely imitated, and thus inaugurate a new era in the history of labor.
But if this signifies approval of a scheme which would immesh our laborers in a net-work of communities owned and managed by industrial superiors, then let every patriotic American cry, God forbid! What would this
mean? The establishment of the most absolute power of capital, and the
repression of all freedom. It matters not that they are well-meaning capitalists; all capitalists are not devoted heart and soul to the interests of their
employés, and the history of the world has long ago demonstrated that
no class of men are fit to be intrusted with unlimited power. In the hour
of temptation and pressure it is abused, and the real nature of the abuse
may for a time be concealed even from him guilty of it; but it degrades
the dependent, corrupts the morals of the superior, and finally that is done
unblushingly in the light which was once scarcely allowed in a dark
corner.

[28.] *"They Only Got 3 or 4 Cents After Paying Their Rent"*

Thomas W. Heathcoate, president of local union No. 208 of
the American Railway Union, tells of conditions leading to
the Pullman strike. [United States Strike Commission, *Report
on the Chicago Strike of June-July, 1894,* Senate Executive
Document No. 7, 53d Cong., 3 sess., 1894-95 (Washington,
D. C.: United States Government Printing Office, 1895), pp.
416-18, 420-26.]

Commissioner WRIGHT. State your name, age, residence, and occupation.
—*Answer.* My name is Thomas W. Heathcoate; am 58 years of age; am

a car builder, and reside at Pullman, Ill.; have been a car builder thirty years; I was employed at the Pullman shops until the recent strike; have been at Pullman as a car builder five years; am a member of the American Railway Union and have been since April, 1894; am president of local union, No. 208, at Pullman; the membership of that local union is 656; there are nineteen local unions of the American Railway Union at Pullman, and their membership varies from 200 to 650 members; I could not state the number of members in each local union exactly; these local unions at Pullman are all affiliated with the American Railway Union.

Commissioner WRIGHT. It has been stated here that the recent strike at Pullman by the employees of the Pullman Palace Car Company was declared by the local unions there belonging to the American Railway Union; is that correct?—*Answer.* Yes, sir.

Commissioner WRIGHT. State what you know of the causes which led to that strike by the local unions at Pullman, the conditions which surrounded it, and any facts connected with it that came within your knowledge. State it in narrative form in your own way, as briefly as possible.—*Answer.* In May, 1893, we were getting good wages and had quite a good deal of work on hand in the Pullman shops; along about September, 1893, our wages began to be reduced because work was slack, that is, on their own work, and they kept reducing our pay each month on almost every contract we took from the company; they kept reducing the price of piece-work until it was almost impossible for us to live; in January, 1894, the men wanted to strike, but we were not organized at that time; there was no organization in the shops, except the painters, and in order to succeed in securing a higher rate of pay it became necessary for us to organize in some way; we could not see any more feasible plan than to organize in the American Railway Union, for the reason, we believed, that union was stronger than any other organization in the country.

Along about the latter part of March or 1st of April, 1894, we began to organize, and in order to do so we had to go to Grand Crossing, as the Pullman company would not tolerate any union in their shops. If a man belonged to a union, if the company knew it, he was discharged; we had to go down to Grand Crossing for the purpose of organizing the first local union; then we held meetings over in Kensington. At about the first meeting that was held I think about 200 signed their names as members of the American Railway Union. The conditions became worse; in April there was another cut, which made it impossible for us to maintain our families and pay our rent; we had to do something; times were hard and men could not get money enough to move away from Pullman; we did not know really what to do. I used my utmost endeavors to keep the men from striking. I knew the condition of the times, but it was utterly impossible for me to control those who wanted to strike; we then held meetings until we had about 35 per cent of the men organized; and on the 10th of May, after this committee had been down to see the Pullman officials, after they had used every effort with the Pullman company to make some concessions . . . a strike was ordered. . . .

The strike occurred on May 11, 1894, and we then met in Turner Hall and appointed what is called a central strike committee for the purpose of conducting the strike. We then appointed committees to watch the Pullman property, so as to protect it. We had about 300 men stationed at different points for that purpose, thinking perhaps hoodlums would come from Chicago and other places and try to destroy the shops. We kept them there night and day, changing the men, until the United States Government sent troops there. There were about 4,500 men there that had nothing to do, and we took that precaution in order to save the Pullman property, and only withdrew our watchmen after the United States militia came.

Commissioner WRIGHT. Did any violence or destruction of property take place at Pullman?—*Answer.* No, sir.

• • •

Commissioner WRIGHT. Have you made application for reinstatement at Pullman?—*Answer.* No, sir; I have been told that I am blacklisted; they have a blacklist there and I have one of them in my pocket, similar to the one sent out to different railroad companies.

• • •

Commissioner WRIGHT. You say labor organizations were not allowed at Pullman and you had to go elsewhere to organize?—*Answer.* Yes, sir.

• • •

Commissioner WRIGHT. But there was no open order against it?—*Answer.* Not at that time, but now when a man goes to the company for a job they ask him, "Are you a member of the American Railway Union?" "Yes, sir." "Have you got a card?" "Yes, sir." "Give us that card." The card is handed to them and then the applicant signs a paper that he will have nothing to do with the American Railway Union or any other order for five years if he wants a place in the Pullman shops.

• • •

Commissioner WRIGHT. What were the results of the two interviews with Mr. [Thomas H.] Wickes [2nd Vice-President of the Pullman Company] of which you have spoken?—*Answer.* We asked Mr. Wickes if he could in any possible way adjust our wages so we could support our families and pay our rents. We wanted either the wages of 1893, or a reduction of the rent and a raise in our pay sufficient to pay rent and support our families. He said the talk about cutting down the rent was utterly impossible, as they were only making 3½ per cent on their money invested. In regard to raising the wages he said they were losing money. You must understand that nine-tenths of the work done in the Pullman shops is Pullman work; the cars are owned by Pullman, and operated by the company. . . .

•   •   •

Commissioner WRIGHT. If rents had been reduced to any reasonable extent, along with the reduction of wages, would the employees at Pullman have been satisfied?—*Answer.* Yes, sir; if they had reduced the rents in proportion to the reduction of wages.

•   •   •

Commissioner WRIGHT. You asked the Pullman company to submit certain questions to arbitration?—*Answer.* Yes, sir.

Commissioner WRIGHT. State specifically just what points you desired to have arbitrated.—*Answer.* We wanted to lay our grievances in regard to our wages and the rents before a board of arbitration, and whatever decision that board arrived at we were satisfied to submit to. If they had said the rents were right as they were, and we were getting wages enough for the class of work we were doing, the employees of the Pullman Palace Car Company would have submitted to that decision.

Commissioner WRIGHT. How did you propose to have that board constituted?—*Answer.* We wanted to select one man, allow the Pullman company to select another, and let those two select a third.

Commissioner WRIGHT. And you promised the company to abide by the result?—*Answer.* Yes, sir. Now, I want to be understood in this matter; other committees went there for the purpose of asking the Pullman company to arbitrate, and Pullman said they had nothing to arbitrate. Mr. Pullman claimed he was losing money, and then two days afterward declared a dividend of $600,000, and that made the men much more determined to strike. It appeared to the men and it appeared to me—and I claim to have a small amount of intelligence—that if I were losing money I could not possibly declare a dividend of $600,000.

•   •   •

. . . When we left the Pullman service we owed George M. Pullman $70,000 rent, and our pay was such we could not pay our rent and have sufficient to eat. I have known men to drop down by the side of a car when they were working for want of food; and the way I had to work myself, in order to make the amount of money I did, I would frequently have to sit down at 10 o'clock in order to rest until I got strength enough to go on again, and there were hundreds of men in that condition at the Pullman shops when we quit.

• • •

Commissioner WORTHINGTON. Do I understand you to say that all the operatives who live in Pullman and are housekeepers live in houses owned by the Pullman company?—*Answer*. Whenever a man is employed in the Pullman shops he is supposed to live in a Pullman house until the Pullman houses are filled; that has been the case previous to this strike; when a man came to the shops he must live in a Pullman house. He could not live in Roseland unless he owned his own property; he must live in Pullman. I have known men who owned property in Roseland who had to leave their property not rented and come down to Pullman and hire houses in order to fill up the Pullman houses.

• • •

Commissioner KERNAN. You spoke a while ago about owing $70,000 back rent; during how long a period has that accumulated?—*Answer*. The accumulation of the back rent commenced about the 1st of November. I do not think there was a man in the Pullman shops that owed any rent up to November 1, 1893.

Commissioner KERNAN. Do you know what, if any, attempts have been made to collect those rents during the last three or four months?—*Answer*. They have been around twice after the rent within the last three months; there have not been any attempts at eviction as yet; when we used to get our pay our pay was in two checks, one check for the rent, the other for the amount we had left.

Commissioner KERNAN. How would the check be made out for the rent? —*Answer*. It would be made out in full for the current rent; that is, two weeks in advance.

Commissioner KERNAN. Was the check payable to your order?—*Answer*. Yes, and I would have to indorse the rent check.

Commissioner KERNAN. And that check would be good anywhere?— *Answer*. They have a paymaster and a rent collector that goes with him.

Commissioner KERNAN. Could you get the rent check cashed anywhere in town?—*Answer*. Not without I was to keep it and not sign it. If I was in such a condition that I could not pay my rent, or any part of it, of course the law of the State is that I must be paid in full; of course they could not compel me to pay the rent, but if I had only $9 coming to me, or any other amount, the rent would be taken out of my pay; that is, the rent check would be left at the bank and I would have to leave my work in the shop, go over to the bank and have an argument there for a few minutes to get the gentleman to let me have money to live on, and sometimes I would get it and sometimes not. I have seen men with families of eight or nine children to support crying there because they only got 3 or 4 cents after paying their rent; I have seen them stand by the window and cry for money enough to enable them to keep their families; I have been insulted at that window time and time again by the clerks when I tried to get money enough to support my family, even after working every day and overtime. They would want to know why I could not pay my rent up when the average per capita was only 8 cents over the rent, and a man would have to keep a family for two weeks on it. If there is any woman can keep a family on 8 cents apiece, clothe themselves, and appear decent on the streets I would like to see it done.

[29.] *"The United States Troops . . . Began Firing Into the Crowd"*

Ray Stannard Baker, who later earned a reputation as a muckraker, describes an incident after the strike had expanded beyond Pullman. [United States Strike Commission, *Report on the Chicago Strike of June-July, 1894*, Senate Executive Document No. 7, 53d Cong., 3 sess., 1894-95 (Washington, D. C.: United States Government Printing Office, 1895), pp. 368-69.]

Commissioner WRIGHT. State your name, residence, and occupation.— *Answer*. My name is Ray Baker; am a newspaper reporter on the Chicago Record; have been on the Record a little more than two years; was employed by the Record in making observations and writing up the recent difficulties in Chicago, and was present at the time of the firing by the regular troops on the mob at Hammond, Ind., Sunday afternoon about the 7th or 8th of July; I do not remember the exact date. The mob had overturned a number of cars the night before and had turned back a couple of passenger trains. About 1 or 2 o'clock Sunday afternoon the mob began to assemble in the center of town and one of the Pullman cars, which had been partially burned the night before, stood on the side track, and a big, rough-looking fellow, whom the people called "Pat"— I did not learn his last name—led the mob down and they threw two ropes over the top of the Pullman car and made an attempt to overturn it. A large crowd, principally women and children, gathered around and just as the mob was about to overturn the car the United States troops who had been riding up and down the track in a caboose with an engine attached came in view and began firing into the crowd. I was in the center of the crowd myself near the place where they were trying to overturn the Pullman car, and the firing was entirely without warning, without even a shout.

As soon as the firing began, of course the crowd scattered, but it was hemmed in on each side by long rows of box cars which they could not get between very well and so they had to run in the direction of the firing, and a number of men, women, and children were injured, or rather men and women, there were no children, and none of those who were injured were members of the mob that was trying to overturn the Pullman cars. I saw the man who was killed; he stood in the crowd not a great distance from me. He did not have hold of the ropes and he was apparently merely a spectator. The men who did have hold of the ropes were not strikers. I know that, because this big fellow who led the mob I looked up afterwards and found him to be a tough from Chicago. As soon as the riots were over he mounted a beer keg in front of one of the saloons and advised men to go home, get their guns, and come out and fight the troops, fire on them. He repeated the statement over and over again and a number of the men did as they were requested to do. He was the leading spirit, in fact, the only one who made any demonstration. As soon as reenforcements of troops came from the city, Lieutenant Payne made his way into the crowd and drove the fellow off. The same man appeared two nights later at Whiting, Ind., and made quite a disturbance there, roused the people up. In all that mob that had hold of the ropes I do not think there were many American Railway Union men. I think they were mostly roughs from Chicago who had been brought there by the excitement. Hammond is just across in a straight line about 20 or 22 miles from Chicago.

[30.] *"It Was the Principle Involved"*

George M. Pullman, founder and president of Pullman's Palace Car Company, states his position. [United States Strike Commission, *Report on the Chicago Strike of June-July, 1894*, Senate Executive Document No. 7, 53d Cong., 3 sess., 1894-95 (Washington, D. C.: United States Government Printing Office, 1895), pp. 553-54, 564-67.]

Commissioner WORTHINGTON. I wanted to know what you had in mind at the time you made this statement that "it was very clear that no prudent man could submit to arbitration in this matter" when you were referring to your daily losses as a reason why any prudent man could not submit to arbitration?—*Answer*. The amount of the losses would not cut any figure; it was the principle involved, not the amount that would affect my views as to arbitration.

Commissioner WORTHINGTON. Then it was not the amount of losses that the company was then sustaining, but it was the fact that a continuance of the business at the rates that had been paid would entail loss upon the company?—*Answer*. It was the principle that that should not be submitted to a third party. That was a matter that the company should decide for itself.

* * *

Commissioner WORTHINGTON. Now, let me ask you if, taking all the revenues of the Pullman company for the last year, so far as you are advised, if the company has lost money or made money during the last year?—*Answer*. The company has made money during the last year.

Commissioner WORTHINGTON. What amount of dividends was declared during the last year?—*Answer*. The usual dividend of 8 per cent.

Commissioner WORTHINGTON. What is the gross amount?—*Answer*. I can't tell now.

Commissioner WORTHINGTON. It is upwards of $600,000, is it not? It has paid out about $2,800,000 in dividends during the last year, has it not?—*Answer*. It has, for the full year.

* * *

Commissioner WORTHINGTON. Don't you think it would have been right that a corporation that has been so successful financially as the Pullman corporation—and of which we have all been proud—declaring a dividend of $2,800,000, should not have borne some losses for employees who had been working for a long time—shared your profits to that extent with them?—*Answer*. Take the profits to begin with. The manufacturing business at Pullman is a perfectly distinct and separate branch of business from the manufacturing business at Detroit. The profits and losses of that business are kept entirely separate and by itself. I can see no reason why I should take the profit belonging to the 4,200 shareholders and that comes as the result of their investment in this company years ago and pay one set of men a higher rate of wages than I was paying other men in different parts of the country, or than other people were paying men, because the manufacturing business happened to belong to the same company that the business of operating cars did, or that we happened to be able to pay the $2,800,000; because during all the years we have been prudent and put our surplus earnings into property that has helped earn this money, that we should be called upon now to pay them out to give exceptional wages to a certain class of men who happened to be living at Pullman.

•   •   •

Commissioner WORTHINGTON. I understood you to say that in considering the question of wages you would not have any right to take the stockholders' money to give to the men in increasing wages, when you could obtain their labor for less or when it would be at a loss to the company to do so?—*Answer.* I would have no right to take the stockholders' money to give one set of mechanics a higher rate than the market price, or higher than we were paying other men—that is, to give them a contribution, as I understand you to say that if we had made profits, why, divide them. We can only divide profits in a corporation to its stockholders.

Commissioner WORTHINGTON. Let me ask you, then, what right you had to take these contracts at a loss of $400 on a car in order to keep the men at work, if that does not involve exactly the same principle?—*Answer.* No; because there is a business element in that that you will readily understand, that there would be damage resulting to the property of the Pullman company as well as to the men and as to everybody living in that vicinity. If I could by a contribution of money in that way secure the disbursement of $500,000 or $1,000,000, my excuse for it to my stockholders would be that it would save that amount that would otherwise be lost indirectly.

Commissioner WORTHINGTON. A disbursement to whom do you mean?—*Answer.* I mean a disbursement to the wage earners, the supply dealers, and to all the people. I mean that the amount of money involved in those contracts amounted to several hundred thousand dollars. Now, whether the Pullman company got that, or whether it went to Wilmington, Del., or Dayton, Ohio, made a difference with the people living at Pullman, and the disbursement of that money or having no money disbursed—

Commissioner WORTHINGTON. Well, the stockholders would not be interested in the disbursement of money to the wage earners?—*Answer.* The stockholders of the Pullman company would be interested in anything that affected directly or indirectly the value of its property at Pullman.

•   •   •

Commissioner WORTHINGTON. But it would be to the interest of the company to keep the works running, would it not?—*Answer.* But we can't keep them running unless we get work to do, unless the railroad companies want cars and will pay for them. This is as serious a question as it was a year ago. I should be very glad if I could guarantee the men work at Pullman now, that they could be kept on at the wages they are working for now.

Commissioner WORTHINGTON. Provided they do not join the American Railway Union?—*Answer*. I do not think they will, because I think they have had all of the American Railway Union they want. If they had accepted my advice at that time and stayed with us they would have had $350,000 wages paid to them between that time and this, and, as I understand by the papers, between $19,000 and $20,000 have been contributed in a charitable way. That would have been their condition between then and now.

Commissioner KERNAN. The stopping of such large works as yours involves a very great loss to stockholders, does it not?—*Answer*. As a matter of course. This strike has been—

Commissioner KERNAN. No; I mean the shutting down and the stopping of the works is an injury to the stockholders?—*Answer*. Well, of course it means that when the works are shut down they are not earning interest on their cost, and it means the cost of watchmen—

Commissioner KERNAN. I mean, it is an injury in this, that the plant itself deteriorates?—*Answer*. No, sir; not especially.

Commissioner KERNAN. That the cost of keeping up the machinery in repair and taking care of it is a dead loss during the time that it is idle?—*Answer*. Yes; but it does not cost us much to keep the machinery in repair.

Commissioner KERNAN. Yes; but it is a loss for which there is no return?—*Answer*. Yes, sir.

Commissioner KERNAN. And the scattering of the force of help involves a loss in getting them to work again systematically, and so that work is done economically and well; is not that true?—*Answer*. Yes, sir; that is true.

Commissioner KERNAN. Now, then, when you offered to make a reduction on those contracts, as you have stated, did you not have in view the saving of that loss to the stockholders as one of the motives that influenced you?—*Answer*. Yes, sir; I had in view—

Commissioner KERNAN. And you also had in view the natural desire to keep the help at work?—*Answer*. Yes, sir; that appealed to me very strongly. I felt that I wanted, if it was a possible thing, to keep half or two-thirds of the people employed at Pullman during this depression.

Commissioner KERNAN. Now, both of the motives that I have stated appealed to you in deciding to take some contracts at less than cost?—*Answer*. Yes, sir.

Commissioner KERNAN. When this reduction of wages was made was your salary reduced and that of the other officers?—*Answer*. No, sir.

Commissioner KERNAN. Were the salaries of the superintendents and foremen reduced?—*Answer*. No, sir.

Commissioner KERNAN. Now, let me ask you why, in this general reduction, that was not done?—*Answer*. Because it is not easy for the manager of a corporation to find men to fill the positions. Men that have been with a corporation for twenty-five years, it don't lie with me to go to him and say to him, "I am going to reduce your salary $1,000," because he will say, "Very well; you will find somebody else to take my place." And there are very few officers of a corporation, comparatively, to the number of employees, and they are able to command their salaries. It would be a matter of agreement whether they would take less, and it is a matter, then, whether a corporation could afford to dispense with their services.

Commissioner KERNAN. In other words, a corporation could not afford to make a reduction of their salaries?—*Answer*. It would be impossible for me, as the president of a corporation, to reduce the salaries of my officers arbitrarily, because I would find myself possibly without them.

Commissioner KERNAN. You might reduce your own, perhaps, but not theirs.—*Answer*. I might, if I chose, but the difference that it would make on the cost of a car would be so infinitesimal and fractional that it would not be worth considering.

[31.] *"We Have No Recognized Influence in Society"*

Eugene V. Debs, president of the American Railway Union, eloquently voices some grievances of labor. [United States Strike Commission, *Report on the Chicago Strike of June-July, 1894*, Senate Executive Document No. 7, 53d Cong., 3 sess., 1894-95 (Washington, D. C.: United States Government Printing Office, 1895), pp. 156-57, 162-63, 169, 174.]

Commissioner WRIGHT. Have you any further statements to make with reference to the narrative of events occurring here in Chicago during the recent troubles . . . ?—*Answer*. Yes, sir; I would like to say something with reference to the treatment of this matter by the press. I want to say that from the very beginning of this trouble the American Railway Union in its purposes and all its acts has been very grossly misrepresented by some of the leading newspapers of the city of Chicago. Interviews were printed which were not had at all. I want to relate one instance that came under my personal observation which was published here at the time, but may not have been noticed, to show to what extent we were made the victims of a capitalistic press. I think it is a matter the people ought to understand. We have had no way of contradicting falsehoods that have been told about us in the way of counteracting the vicious impression created by false reports.

At the time of the Briggs House meeting a reporter on the Chicago Tribune named Legwig came to me, in the presence of two witnesses, and said, "I have just been discharged." I said, "What for?" He said, "They had me before the grand jury and wanted me to swear to an interview I had with you, and because I would not commit perjury they discharged me." He then showed me an interview—I had had an interview with him, but it was so perverted and distorted in the paper that I did not recognize it as the same interview. He and several other reporters came to me in confidence, and two other members in confidence, and asked us not to have any feeling against them, because after the copy passed from their hands it went into the hopper and came out in a way that made us say things that never were said, and which they were not at all responsible for. We were made to say the most ridiculous and vicious things imaginable that went through the Associated Press, and then the press of the country generally made editorial attacks upon us predicated upon those alleged interviews. . . .

. . . Now, for instance, when I left here to go home it was reported and it went over the Associated Press wires, and I found over 300 letters at my home in Terre Haute in regard to it, that I left here in a Pullman car and waved my adieus from a Pullman car. Then all the press in the country said, "When will you fellows stop following that humbug who appeals to the public not to patronize Pullman cars and then rides away in one himself." Now I did not do that. I have not set foot on a Pullman car since the 11th day of May, 1894. The press all over the country published that I was riding about in Pullman cars. What was the purpose? It was to arouse the prejudice of the public against me because I happened to stand for labor, to destroy the confidence of labor in me, to set me up as a huge fraud and humbug. Then they published that when the train that I was in arrived at Danville an angry railroad striker accused me of being responsible for the loss of his job and struck me. There was not a word of truth in that statement. These are two instances of thousands of statements published all over this country, for no other reason except to prejudice the minds of the public against the officers of the American Railway Union.

•   •   •

Commissioner KERNAN. What is your conclusion as to the best way of avoiding strikes, either by legislation or otherwise?—*Answer*. I was going to make this point first. If railroad corporations and other corporations and employers of labor generally had treated their employees fairly and justly I doubt if there would today be a labor organization in existence. . . .

•   •   •

Just before this trouble I had a conversation with the president of one of the roads, and he said to me: "Now is the time when you can make yourself, in the estimation of the railroad employers, and the railroad employees as well." I said, "In what way?" He said, "You have a certain influence with railroad employees; I advise you to go before them and advise them to voluntarily take a reduction; in fact, to ask for it in view of the hard times. Advise them to come to the front of their own accord; then you put the company under obligation to restore those reduced wages as soon as business revives." I said, "That is a very nice proposition. Only a few months ago your road was doing an overwhelming business, and within my own knowledge your road has been making a great deal of money. Did it ever occur to you in your prosperous times to go to your employees and say: 'Here, men, we are making a good deal of money; we believe you ought to share our prosperity with us and we are going to increase your wages on and after the 1st of June 5 per cent.' Did you ever do that? Do you know of any manager that ever did that?" He said he could not recall any case of that kind. I said, "Neither can I." I said, "In your prosperous times it never occurred to you to voluntarily give to your employees what they were entitled to, and you have no right to expect that they will voluntarily come to you and ask to have their wages reduced. If you had set an example in that way and inspired their confidence and a necessary reduction was made they would bear it like men, because you had treated them fairly when prosperous. But the railroad companies never did that; they only make concessions when compelled to, and that is a fact that is easily proved."

. . . If the present conditions continue it is only a question of time until there will be other strikes. There are some people, and many good people, who felicitate themselves upon the fact that this strike has been suppressed and general quiet has been restored, but they are very much mistaken; they have simply screwed down the safety valve; the men have submitted because they were compelled to, but they are no more satisfied than they were at the time the strike was inaugurated. A good many of them are out of work and will find it very hard, I have no doubt, to find other employment. But they will pay all the penalty by enforced idleness; they will find work after awhile; some of them under other names will get back to work again, but they will not be content by any means.

In the meantime the managers will do everything they can to squelch the American Railway Union, but it will be impossible; they might as well try to stop Niagara with a feather as to crush the spirit of organization in this country. It can not be done. It may not come up in the form of the American Railway Union, but this spirit of resistance to wrong is there, it is growing stronger constantly, and, it finds its outlet in labor disturbances, in strikes of various kinds. Even if the men know in advance that they are going to meet with defeat they are so impressed with a sense of wrong under which they are suffering that they strike and take the penalty. You ask what I would do, or what my ideas are about what should be done to avert strikes. To avert railroad strikes I would propose this: "That Government ownership of railroads is decidedly better for the people than railroad ownership of Government." [Applause.]

. . .

We have always said we were in favor of arbitrating every difficulty. Every proposal we have made in that direction has been rejected with scorn. We have nothing to look forward to to defend us in times of trouble. We have only got a number, and a limited number, of poorly paid men in our organization, and when their income ceases they are starving. We have no power of the Government behind us. We have no recognized influence in society on our side. We have absolutely nothing but the men who begin to starve when they quit work. On the other side the corporations are in perfect alliance; they have all of the things that money can command, and that means a subsidized press, that they are able to control the newspapers, and means a false or vitiated public opinion. The clergy almost steadily united in thundering their denunciations; then the courts, then the State militia, then the Federal troops; everything and all things on the side of corporations. When the authorities are called upon to intercede in troubles of this kind do they ever ask labor a question? Never. They always go to where capital sits in council and there receive their orders as I view it—do what they command shall be done.

We have had a great many conflicts in this country between capital and labor. We know by experience and by the truth of history that in a great many of those conflicts the workingmen were right. We know that their wages were unjustly reduced and their rights trampled down. When and where did the militia ever come out and take its stand on the side of labor, to prevent the workingmen's being robbed and degraded? Never. Whenever and wherever they have been called out it was always to take their place on the side of the capitalist. They have gone into partnership with the oppressors of labor to crush labor. If there was a perfect sense of duty and justice prevailing at the proper places they would not have to exercise their powers as they now do, always with the one purpose of crushing the workingmen. They could enforce the demands of justice without any additional legislation on the subject, in my opinion; but the moneyed power, it seems to me, is potential enough to control all this machinery, and will be able to do it with the additional legislation that you propose, in my opinion.

•   •   •

Commissioner WRIGHT. In another answer you spoke of militia being called out always to protect the employer as against the striking employee, or words to that effect. Is it not a fact that the militia is always called out to protect property, whether it belongs to the employer or to the employee, and not to take sides with either party?—*Answer.* I should not think that were the fact, after General Miles' statement that he had broken the backbone of the strike.

Commissioner WRIGHT. That is an individual matter. I refer to the calling out of the militia?—*Answer.* Let me recite this as a statement of fact: In 1892, if I remember rightly, the State of New York passed a law that provided that ten hours should constitute a day's work. That had been passed for some time, and the switchmen who were working at Buffalo were compelled to work from twelve to fourteen hours a day, notwithstanding the legislature of New York had passed a law providing that ten hours should constitute a day's work. The switchmen appointed committees, who called on the officials of the several roads centering at Buffalo—the New York Central, the Erie, the Lehigh Valley, and the rest of them. Those officials would not treat with the committee at all, and as a last resort the switchmen, about 600 in number, struck. Mr. Theodore Voorhees, then superintendent and latterly general manager of the Lehigh Valley, wrote a paper on that strike, which appeared in the North American Review of August, I believe, of that year, in which he practically admitted that the railroad corporations had combined for the purpose of disregarding that ten-hour law.

When the switchmen struck they paralyzed all of the roads centering at Buffalo. There was no riot, no disorder, and no trouble, but the roads could not get men to handle the work. There were some cars on the hospital track—old and disabled cars—and they were set on fire. That looked very suspicious, to say the least, and it was currently reported at that time, and I believe it to be the fact, that those cars were fired by the emissaries of the corporations, because what interest could the switchmen possibly have had in firing those decrepit, disabled cars? The very instant those cars were fired the mayor of Buffalo called on the governor of New York and says, "Buffalo is in flames." Six thousand soldiers promptly responded, and there was no cause for them—not the slightest—but 6,000 soldiers responded, the courts responded, and those 600 switchmen were squelched. The 600 switchmen were asking for nothing except that the corporations live up to the law passed by the legislature. Yet they were suppressed by the soldiers. The soldiers were used to suppress switchmen who were simply contending for the enforcement of law. The soldiers came out and stood by the corporations, which were violating the law, and crushed the switchmen, who were contending for the enforcement of the law.

V

IMMIGRATION

Many laborers, particularly unskilled laborers, were immigrants. Economic opportunities for both skilled and unskilled laborers were much greater in America than in Europe. American racial, ethnic, and religious prejudice and bigotry were infinitely preferable to the rigid class structure and grinding poverty of Eastern and Southern Europe or to being murdered by the Czar's Christian subjects during a pogrom. America's democracy, political freedom, and small army appealed to liberals who wished to exchange subjugation to an autocratic, repressive, and militaristic regime for citizenship in a free republic.

Although some migrants, particularly from Northern Europe, had sufficient capital and inclination to farm, most immigrants moved not merely from Europe to America but also from country to city. The city offered greater economic opportunities—opportunities, moreover, that required little or no outlay of capital. But most immigrants could secure only "foreign jobs"—the hardest, dirtiest, most dangerous and worst paying tasks.

The saga of the immigrant—his difficult voyage, the unfriendly reception, his frequently being cheated by his better-established countrymen, his undesirable job, and his dreadful slum quarters—has been passionately recounted by himself and his children. That immigrant muscle, bone, and blood helped build America cannot be denied, but the emotional claim that cultural contributions of Gilded Age immigrants were significant is debatable. Immigrants and their children found it easier to adjust to their new surroundings than to change American society. The public school and the political party helped assimilate them into American life. While old world cultural patterns disappeared, the prejudices of American society reinforced ties between people of the same ethnic background.

Though mere traces of alien cultures remain, the political effect of these ethnic ties is very much with us today.

[32.] *"To Live Among Strangers in a Strange Land"*

The American Social Science Association cautions the would-be immigrant on the serious step he is contemplating. [American Social Science Association, *Handbook for Immigrants to the United States* (New York: Hurd and Houghton, 1871), p. 1.]

There can hardly be a more serious act than a change of country. To emigrate is to take a step, of which neither the most hopeful nor the most thoughtful can correctly foresee the full consequences, for good or for evil. It means nothing less than to part for years, if not forever, with home, relations, and friends; to break up old and dear habits; to live among strangers in a strange land; to recommence, often from the very beginning, the struggle of life.

[33.] *"Doing Work Which Americans Instinctively Shrink From"*

Lafcadio Hearn describes the slaughter-house district of Cincinnati populated by "a foreign population, speaking a foreign tongue." [Lafcadio Hearn, "The Quarter of Shambles," *Cincinnati Enquirer* (November 15, 1874), in Lafcadio Hearn, *Occidental Gleanings*, ed. Albert Mordell (New York: Dodd, Mead & Company, 1925), pp. 67-68. Reprinted by permission of Dodd, Mead & Company.]

. . . It is a quarter where the senses of sight and hearing and smell are at once assailed with all the foulnesses of the charnel-house and the shambles. It is the center of all those trades which harden and brutalize the men who engage in them. Its gutters run with ordure and blood; its buildings reek with smells of slaughter and stenches abominable beyond description. An atmosphere heavy with the odors of death and decay and animal filth and steaming nastiness of every description, hangs over it like the sickly smoke of an ancient holocaust. In fact, it has an atmosphere peculiar to itself, whose noisome stagnation is scarcely disturbed on the breeziest days by a clear fresh current of heaven's purer air. Mammoth slaughter-houses, enormous rendering establishments, vast soap and candle factories, immense hog-pens and gigantic tanneries loom up through the miasmatic atmosphere for blocks and blocks in every direction. Narrow alleys, dark and filthy, bordered by sluggish black streams of stinking filth, traverse this quarter in every direction. The main streets here lose their width and straightness in tortuous curves and narrow twists and labyrinthine perplexity—so that the stranger who loses his way in this region of nastiness must wander wildly and long ere he may cease to inhale the ghoulish aroma of stink-factories and the sickening smell of hog-pens fouler than the stables of Augeas. Night-carts, which elsewhere leave far behind them a wake of stench suggestive of epidemics, here may pass through in broad daylight without betraying their presence. Rats propagate undisturbed and grow fat and gigantic among the dung-piles and offal-dumps. Amid these scenes and smells lives and labors a large and strangely healthy population of brawny butchers, sinewy coopers, muscular tanners—a foreign population, speaking a foreign tongue, and living the life of the Fatherland—broad-shouldered men from Pomerania; tall, fair-haired emigrants from Bohemia; dark, brawny people from Bavaria; rough-featured fellows from the region of the Hartz Mountains; men speaking the strange dialects of strange provinces. They are mostly rough of aspect, rude of manner and ruddy of feature. The greater part of them labor in tanneries, slaughter-houses and soap factories, receiving small salaries upon which an American workman could not support his family, and doing work which Americans instinctively shrink from —slaughtering, quartering, flaying—handling bloody entrails and bloody hides—making slaughter their daily labor, familiarizing themselves with death and agony, and diurnally drenching themselves in blood. Such occupation destroys the finer sensibilities of men, and more or less brutalizes their natures; while in return it gives them health and strength and brawn beyond the average. The air they breathe is indeed foully odorous, but it is heavily rich with globules of fresh blood and tallow and reeking flesh— healthy for the lungs and veins of the breathers.

[34.] *"An Undigested Lump"*

James B. Reynolds, head worker of New York City's Univer-
sity Settlement Society, reports to the Industrial Commission.
[*Report of the Industrial Commission on the Relations and
Conditions of Capital and Labor . . . ,* Commission's Reports
Vol. XIV (Washington, D. C.: United States Government
Printing Office, 1901), 81-82, 92-94.]

Question. (By Mr. CLARKE). Speak, if you please, of the nationalities
and the occupations, and in fact all the surroundings of the people who
are affiliated with your work.—*Answer.* Well, in the 14 years that we
have been there we have had a glimpse of the rather curious procession
of races which has marched up New York City during the last 40 years.
As is probably known to you, 50 years ago the quarter just east of the
Bowery was an American quarter and the dwelling place of some of the
wealthy families of the city; but about that time the Irish immigration
began, and the Irish pushed the Americans uptown.

Following the Irish came the Germans; and the Germans, by their
rather more careful and more thrifty methods of life, drove the Irish
uptown. The Irish had become fairly well settled and understood the
conditions of the country and were better able to look out for themselves,
and they moved up.

Following the Germans, about the time that we established our settlement, say in 1877, came the Jewish immigration—the Russian and Polish
Jew. They crowded the Germans out. When we began, our immediate
district was almost equally divided between the Jewish and the German
population. But the work of exclusion of the German population has
gone steadily on until that quarter is practically monopolized by Russian
and Polish and Armenian Jews. There is a large public school opposite
our building, and the principal told me recently that from 97 to 98 per
cent were Jewish children, and the same is true of several other schools
in our immediate vicinity.

There is now developing the next product of this social army, namely,
the Italian immigration. Within the last 3 years they have begun to press
into the quarter; coming from across the Bowery in Mulberry street,
where they are established in large numbers, and pushing east in our
direction and west into the west side where our other settlement is located.

If you follow the city down a little farther you will find small detach-
ments of Syrians and Greeks and Armenians; but that is about the procession of immigration we have had occasion to witness in the last 10 or 15
years. Now the population is largely Russian, Polish, and Armenian Jews.
The persecution of the Roumanians in the last few years has sent large
bodies of the Roumanians into this country, and they are crowding at
present into our quarter.

•   •   •

Question. (By Mr. LITCHMAN). . . . Will you kindly give to the commission your ideas upon immigration . . . ?—*Answer.* . . . The first
fact I would like to notice regarding immigration is its effect on the
character of the immigrants where large masses of them come over in a
body, and settle in one quarter of the city. We all know, I think, that the
question of the poor quarter of an American city is the question of some
of our foreign races. I have not found a poor quarter of any American
city which is an American quarter. Now, then, what one does notice when
he comes to these foreign quarters of an American city is that the immigrants have come, say, from Russia, Germany, Poland, and Italy, and
have settled in this country in a mass. They form an undigested lump.
That lump, because it is a lump, is very much more slowly digested in the
American life than it would be if it were more scattered. . . . Large
masses of foreign populations form substantially foreign colonies in our
midst. In some of our quarters, for instance, the regular holiday is Saturday and not Sunday, and garment workers, not by hundreds but thousands,
work on Sunday, and the language is German or the Jewish jargon in
one section and Italian in another section. Now, it would seem a wise and
intelligent policy on the part of the American National Government and
State governments and the city governments to . . . send . . . the best
and strongest forces to work in those quarters of our large cities. Instead
of that, what do we find now. Take the public schools as an illustration.
We find that the brightest teachers as a rule seek the uptown schools.
We find the best school buildings in New York are in the most comfortable quarters of the city. We find the best school equipment will be in
connection with those better schools; and though you find exceptions,
where teachers of the very best caliber will as a matter of personal self-
denial go into the poorer quarters of the city, nevertheless you do not
find any steady policy in any city I know on the part of school superintendents to send their strongest teachers and principals to these districts
where the work of education is going to be carried on under the greatest
difficulties, any policy to see that the very best schoolhouses are established, where the schoolhouses will be about the only clean, sanitary, and

well-lighted buildings in these districts. We do not find any steady policy of seeing that those schools are supplied with the best material for work, so that the school shall be at its very best. In all the other departments of our State government this state of affairs is found. I do not reflect on the officers, because there are in each case exceptions, but as a rule the better officials operate in the better districts, and there is no systematic, intelligent, steady policy pursued of sending the best officials and pursuing the most careful work of municipal education and municipal reform in the districts where there is the least opportunity, the least privilege, and the greatest need; and the failure of our government to do this seems to me the most lamentable failure we are making with the poor at the present time. . . .

•   •   •

Mr. Chairman, I would like to make a very brief supplementary statement. I would like to generalize, first, that in our poorer quarters there is a most unfortunate lack of equality or opportunity as compared with the opportunities offered to the better-conditioned classes. I have been impressed in my residence of 7 years in the lower quarter of New York City that while the material conditions are most unfortunate, and the victims of them are great sufferers, nevertheless the moral and intellectual poverty of the people is even greater than the material poverty.

There is in the poorer quarters of our cities an utter absence of privileges which help to make life enjoyable and wholesome in other quarters of the city. I have called attention to the defect of education. I should specify also the defect in the supply of lavatory privileges. I have called attention to the evils of the pawnshop and the disadvantages to which the people are subjected by the pawnshops. I might also name the general disadvantages which appear in all their commercial workshops.

We at the university settlement have our own house, and there are 10 of us living in that house. We can go to a grocer's establishment, a butcher's, or a general-supplies establishment in another part of the city and get a better grade of goods at cheaper rates than the people of our quarter can buy in their quarter, and we are therefore in better circumstances and in better condition at a less price than are the people about us—our neighbors of the district. I call attention to this fact because I want to emphasize the unfortunate condition of those whom we are trying to Americanize, and whom we owe it to ourselves to Americanize.

I would like also to call attention to the Italian community. It is said that there are from 150,000 to 200,000 in the Greater New York. I have noted the sweat shop as one evil appearing in that community. The private bank is the second evil generally known and recognized. A man establishes a small private bank; he dictates the correspondence of a certain number of immigrants whom he knows and manages their affairs for them. Suddenly some morning they find he has gone; he has left with all the deposits. That bank is a peculiar evil preying upon the Italian community. The Italian Government, I am informed, has gone so far as to ask its agents to make an investigation of that evil, and is considering the establishment of a branch of the Italian Bank in New York City. The reason the Italian Government is doing this is because a part of the Italian population sends back its money to Italy, and thereby helps to pay the taxes of the Italian Government. If the Italian Government is willing to do this in the interest of the minor part of the Italian population in this country for their own gain, it seems to me that we, in the interest of the major part, who are going to become permanent citizens of our country, have still far greater considerations at stake.

The third evil is the padrone system, the small subcontractor of labor, an evil which is so generally known that one even hesitates to name it.

I wish to call attention to those three evils. The evils spring up in this country because the people come as I have said in large masses, utterly ignorant of the conditions in our country, and subject to exploitation by every villain of their own race who is willing to take advantage of their ignorance and inexperience.

[35.] *"Distinctly on the Upward Road"*

Kate Holladay Claghorn, a specialist on immigration, compares Italian immigrants with other immigrant groups. [Kate Holladay Claghorn, "Foreign Immigration and the Tenement House in New York City," in *The Tenement House Problem,* ed. Robert W. DeForest and Lawrence Veiller (New York: The Macmillan Company, 1903), II, 84-87.]

Italians were noticeable elements of population in the sixth ward, the quarter of the Five Points, as far back as 1864. The early comers were largely rag-pickers and organ-grinders, and many children were brought here under padroni to beg, to shine boots and shoes, and sell newspapers, or to go about with the hand-organ in the streets.

Between 1879 and 1885 frequent mention is made of Italian neighborhoods in the northern part of the fourteenth ward, just below Houston Street. A colony in Jersey Street, running from Crosby Street to Mulberry, just south of Houston, . . . was especially noticed. It is thus described in 1884 :—

> In Jersey Street exist two courtyards. . . . Six three-story houses are in each. These houses are old, and long ago worn out. They are packed with tenants, rotten with age and decay, and so constructed as to have made them very undesirable for dwelling purposes in their earliest infancy. The Italians who chiefly inhabit them are the scum of New York chiffonniers, and as such, saturated with the filth inseparable from their business. . . . The courtyard swarms with, in daytime, females in the picturesque attires of Genoa and Piedmont, moving between the dirty children. The abundant rags, paper, sacks, barrows, barrels, wash-tubs, dogs, and cats, are all festooned overhead by clothes-lines weighted with such garments as are only known in Italy. Sorting is chiefly done indoors, but at times a rag-picker may be seen at his work in any convenient spot to be had. . . . In each yard live twenty-four families (nominally only, because lodgers here as elsewhere are always welcome), paying rents of from $6 to $9 monthly for two rooms, the inner one being subdivided by a partition consisting perhaps of a simple curtain, and measuring, when so arranged, about 5 × 6 feet each.

An earlier report . . . made in 1879, gives the following additional touches of description :—

> Here in the yard of No. 5 Jersey Street, on lines strung across, were thousands of rags hung up to dry; on the ground, piled against the board fences, rags mixed with bones, bottles, and papers; the middle of the yard covered with every imaginable variety of dirt. . . . We then turned to go into the cellars, in which was a large and a small room (containing a cook-stove and sleeping-bunks). There was scarcely standing room for the heaps of bags and rags, and right opposite to them stood a large pile of bones, mostly having meat on them in various stages of decomposition. . . . Notwithstanding the dense tobacco smoke, the smell could be likened only to that of an exhumed body.

* * *

It hardly needs to be pointed out how closely these descriptions of the early type of Italian immigrants parallel what was told us of the German "chiffonnier" population of the forties and fifties; and yet to-day the German is looked upon as so many degrees higher in the scale than the Italian that any likeness in original condition between the two is usually overlooked.

In the Italian immigration, following the advance guard of rag-pickers and organ-grinders, came a vast army of unskilled day laborers—practically the same class that the early Irish immigration afforded.

It is, probably, due somewhat to remembrances of the organ-grinding period, that our impression of the Italian is of an idle, roving vagabond. But to-day the laboring class makes up the great majority of the Italian immigrant population, and on the streets and railroads, and in construction work of all kinds, is taking the place occupied by the Irish forty years ago. The Italian laborer and his family may be said, indeed, to be more steady and sober, more provident, more generally reliable than their Irish predecessors. Untidy in their habits they undoubtedly are, although not so much so as the rag-pickers who preceded them. But landlords bear testimony to their promptness in paying rent, and to their general good care of the premises they occupy—that is, to the absence of the special gift of destructiveness that seemed to incite the Irish tenant to break everything breakable about a place.

There are not wanting indications to show that the Italian immigrant population will not be the dead weight in our tenement districts that they have been thought likely to be. While the newly arrived immigrant is a day laborer, or a peddler, his son is likely to want to be something else. Italians are found keeping small shops in every quarter of the city,—for fruit, wine, groceries, candy, ice-cream, etc. They keep cafés and restaurants and dry-goods stores; are shoemakers, watchmakers, and barbers. The Italian boot-black has distinctly elevated his occupation, bringing to it better appointments, a higher standard of work, and a certain pride in keeping up to standards that makes this almost an artistic profession. Even the fruit peddlers "compose" their wares in harmonies of color and arrangement that show an instinct of order and beauty which must certainly come to something under favoring circumstances.

•   •   •

The Hebrew immigrant, like the Italian, is poor, is unclean in his personal habits, will submit to excessive overcrowding when he first comes over; but, like the Italian, he is industrious, saving, careful of property. He may in general be counted on to pay rent, but not so certainly, perhaps, as the Italian.

The Italian immigrants are, when they come here, little given to drink or violence; the Hebrews even less so. And the Hebrew, like the Italian, is distinctly on the upward road. It is a common saying among those who are familiar with them that in ten years the Hester Street family has moved up on Lexington Avenue.

Owing partly to accident, partly to differences in racial character, the Italian and Hebrew demands for housing have been met in a somewhat different way. Italians have found their way largely into the parts of the city previously occupied by the Irish—the fourth, sixth, eighth, and fourteenth wards, and have established themselves in the old "front and rear" tenement already abandoned by their Irish occupants, or about to be abandoned in consequence of the incoming of this new people. The Hebrews, on the other hand, are especially associated with the big "double-decker" or "dumb-bell" tenement. These houses were erected in great numbers on the East Side, which was not so fully taken up with the old type of tenement as the wards entered by the Italians; and here the Hebrews made their way, pushing out the Germans as the Italians were pushing out the Irish. In 1892 vast numbers of Hebrews landed here, in consequence of the persecutions in Russia; and the stream has continued in great volume ever since. And since 1892 great numbers of the big "dumb-bells" have been erected, replacing the smaller dwellings, which simply could not, by any degree of crowding, be made to hold the incoming thousands. Colonies both of Italians and Hebrews have been started in Harlem, and there the "dumb-bells" have been erected for both races.

[36.] *"The Prevailing Kind of . . . Tenement House"*

Two experts of the New York State Tenement House Commission describe the building most familiar to New York City immigrants. [*The Tenement House Problem,* ed. Robert W. DeForest and Lawrence Veiller (New York: The Macmillan Company, 1903), I, 7-9.]

Some knowledge of the prevailing kind of New York tenement house must necessarily precede any consideration of its evils and their remedies. It is known as the "double-decker," "dumb-bell" tenement, a type which New York has the unenviable distinction of having invented. . . .

. . . The tall tenement house, accommodating as many as 100 to 150 persons in one building, extending up six or seven stories into the air, with dark, unventilated rooms, is unknown in London or in any other city of Great Britain. It was first constructed in New York about the year 1879, and with slight modifications has been practically the sole type of building erected since, and is the type of the present day. It is a building usually five or six or even seven stories high, about 25 feet wide, and built upon a lot of land of the same width and about 100 feet deep. The building as a rule extends back 90 feet, leaving the small space of ten feet unoccupied at the rear, so that the back rooms may obtain some light and air. This space has continued to be left open only because the law has compelled it. Upon the entrance floor there are generally two stores, one on each side of the building, and these sometimes have two or three living rooms back of them. In the centre is the entrance hallway, a long corridor less than 3 feet wide and extending back 60 feet in length. This hallway is nearly always totally dark. . . . Generally, along each side of the building is what is termed an "air shaft." . . . The ostensible purpose of the shaft is to provide light and air to the five rooms on each side of the house which get no direct light and air from the street or yard; but as the shafts are narrow and high, being enclosed on all four sides, and without any intake of air at the bottom, these rooms obtain, instead of fresh air and sunshine, foul air and semi-darkness. Indeed it is questionable whether the rooms would not be more habitable and more sanitary with no shaft at all, depending for their light and air solely upon the front and back rooms into which they open; for each family, besides having the foul air from its own rooms to breathe, is compelled to breathe the emanations from the rooms of some eleven other families; nor is this all, these shafts act as conveyors of noise, odors, and disease, and when fire breaks out serve as inflammable flues, often rendering it impossible to save the buildings from destruction.

A family living in such a building pays for four rooms of this kind a rent of from $12 to $18 a month. . . . In the public hallway, opposite the stairs, there are provided two water-closets, each water-closet being used in common by two families and being lighted and ventilated by the "air shaft," which also lights and ventilates all the bedrooms.

[37.] *"Once Every Summer"*
the Sun Came In

Jacob A. Riis, an immigrant reporter, publicizes the need of tenement house reform. [Jacob A. Riis, "The Tenement House Blight," *The Atlantic Monthly*, LXXXIII, No. 500 (June 1899), 760-61.]

In a Stanton Street tenement, the other day, I stumbled upon a Polish capmaker's home. There were other capmakers in the house, Russian and Polish, but they simply "lived" there. This one had a home. The fact proclaimed itself the moment the door was opened, in spite of the darkness.

The rooms were in the rear, gloomy with the twilight of the tenement, although the day was sunny without, but neat, even cosy. It was early, but the day's chores were evidently done. The teakettle sang on the stove, at which a bright-looking girl of twelve, with a pale but cheery face, and sleeves brushed back to the elbows, was busy poking up the fire. A little boy stood by the window, flattening his nose against the pane and gazing wistfully up among the chimney pots where a piece of blue sky about as big as the kitchen could be made out. I remarked to the mother that they were nice rooms.

"Ah yes," she said, with a weary little smile that struggled bravely with hope long deferred, "but it is hard to make a home here. We would so like to live in the front, but we can't pay the rent."

I knew the front with its unlovely view of the tenement street too well, and I said a good word for the air shaft—yard or court it could not be called, it was too small for that—which rather surprised myself. I had found few virtues enough in it before. The girl at the stove had left off poking the fire. She broke in the moment I finished, with eager enthusiasm: "Why, they have the sun in there. When the door is opened the light comes right in your face."

"Does it never come here?" I asked, and wished I had not done so, as soon as the words were spoken. The child at the window was listening, with his whole hungry little soul in his eyes.

Yes, it did, she said. Once every summer, for a little while, it came over the houses. She knew the month and the exact hour of the day when its rays shone into their home, and just the reach of its slant on the wall. They had lived there six years. In June the sun was due. A haunting fear that the baby would ask how long it was till June—it was February then— took possession of me, and I hastened to change the subject. Warsaw was their old home. They kept a little store there, and were young and happy. Oh, it was a fine city, with parks and squares, and bridges over the beautiful river,—and grass and flowers and birds and soldiers, put in the girl breathlessly. She remembered. But the children kept coming, and they went across the sea to give them a better chance. Father made fifteen dollars a week, much money; but there were long seasons when there was no work. She, the mother, was never very well here,—she had n't any strength; and the baby! She glanced at his grave white face, and took him in her arms. The picture of the two, and of the pale-faced girl longing back to the fields and the sunlight, in their prison of gloom and gray walls, haunts me yet. I have not had the courage to go back since. I recalled the report of an English army surgeon, which I read years ago, on the many more sol- diers that died—were killed would be more correct—in barracks into which the sun never shone than in those that were open to the light. It is yet three months to the sun in Stanton Street.

[38.] *"Part of the Great General Movement . . . to the City"*

Kate Holladay Claghorn compares the "new immigrant" with the "old immigrant" and contrasts his few opportunities in the country with his numerous ones in the city. [Kate Holladay Claghorn, "The Foreign Immigrant in New York City," in *Report of the Industrial Commission on Immigration . . . ,* Commission's Reports Vol. XV (Washington, D. C.: United States Government Printing Office, 1901), 491-92.]

On the whole, it does not seem that the newer immigration offers any greater or more serious problems than the old, except in so far as they add to the total numbers and increase the general overcrowding.

In the newer period general health conditions have certainly improved. There is no more of the sickness among immigrants due to unsanitary conditions on the passage over. Under the present immigration regulations only immigrants of fair physical condition are admitted to the country. In the city, notwithstanding bad tenement conditions that might be improved, the general death rate has fallen greatly since the fifties, due to a more enlightened sanitary system.

The newer immigrants arrive here at no lower social level, to say the least, than did their predecessors. Their habits of life, their general morality and intelligence can not be called decidedly inferior. No account of filth in daily surroundings among Italians and Hebrews can outmatch the pictures drawn by observers of the habits of immigrant Irish and even Germans. The Italian ragpicker was astonishingly like his German predecessor, and the Italian laborer is of quite as high a type as the Irish laborer of a generation ago.

In some cases the newer immigrants have brought about positive improvement in the quarters they have entered. Whole blocks have been transformed from nests of pauperism and vice into quiet industrial neighborhoods by the incoming of Italians and Hebrews.

Simple overcrowding, however, is an evil in itself, and when this takes place it becomes desirable to encourage tendencies toward movement out of the cities on the part of immigrants. . . .

It should be remembered in making plans for the dispersion of immigrants how strong are certain inducements of real and genuine advantage for them to remain in a large city. That there are advantages offered in cities is shown by the fact that the native born are flocking there as well as the foreign born. The immigrants' journey across the ocean is as much a part of the great general movement from the country to the city going on all over the world for some years as is the journey of the American lad from the country town to the city.

Primarily, the city is the great industrial center. The principal occupation to be found by the immigrant in country districts—agricultural labor—must probably be regarded as, on the whole, less remunerative than any other. . . .

•   •   •

An allowance of actual yearly earnings for each person in each class (taking count of unemployment) would be, on this basis, as follows:

Agricultural laborers	$215
Domestic and personal servants	227
Trade and transportation	340
Lumbermen, quarrymen, etc.	372
Miners	420
Manufacturing and mechanical industries	445

In the cities, mainly, are to be found the opportunities for the higher paid employments, and the larger the city the greater the number of openings. It is quite true that the supply of labor may be greater than the demand in the larger market; but in the larger market each individual sees more chances at least of employment and thinks that he is as likely to be one of those lucky enough to secure them as any other.

Other advantages offered by cities are substantial ones to the immigrant. In the cities are the various institutions for the help and comfort of the poor that provide what they can not easily provide for themselves—the hospitals, dispensaries, charitable societies, schools, libraries, social settlements, and all such things.

Before the immigrant is too severely condemned for lingering in the cities such considerations as these should be taken into account.

[39.] *"As Foreign As Any Foreign Land"*

Gist Blair tours the foreign sections of New York on an
Easter weekend. Although this letter was written in 1906,
everything it states could have been said at the close of the
Gilded Age. In 1899, for instance, New York City opened
up thirty-one playgrounds. [Gist Blair (son of Montgomery
Blair) to his aunts Virginia Woodbury Fox and Ellen De-
Quincy Woodbury (New York, Easter Sunday [1906]), Blair
Family Papers, Library of Congress, Washington, D. C. Al-
though the year is not given, this letter can be dated pre-
cisely since it refers to a recent death in the family.]

I am visiting my old friend Alec Butler Duncan who is lolling on a sofa
in this sweet old fashioned room while I scribble to you. . . .

Yesterday we were at the Rockaway Hunt Club on Long Island where
I rode a couple of polo ponies, & last night we returned to dine at the
Players Club, just he & I, & wander through the Hungarian settlement of
New York until the wee small hours of the morning. Little Hungary—
like little Italy—is as foreign as any foreign land I have seen. Signs at
the theatres that announce the plays are in Yiddish, people chatter in
many languages and at one o'clock the stores were still open & beef steaks
and vegetables & cotton & shoes being sold to an orderly public. Our
night was not in the streets alone. We passed several hours drinking
Hungarian wine at their principal garden where Mr. Schwartz the proprietor talked with us. The music superb. The members of the band took turns
singing at times introducing an actor's part to more fully explain their
songs—the audience joined or not as emotions influenced them. The men
& women were orderly at all times but no gentleman seemed to hesitate
about giving a kiss to his fair partner because of those who surrounded
him.

●   ●   ●

. . . My interest over last night's experience started Alec into showing
me other scenes from N. Y. It being Easter we expected to find much & we
have done so. He ordered his buggy and we two started after luncheon
& are just back having been two hours inspecting the Jewish quarter, the
Italian quarter, the Chinese quarter, & the Irish quarter. In the last alone
did we see the least show of bad manners, or of lawlessness. Our horse

was struck twice by mud or stones & two small girls were fighting in the Irish quarter. One travels to see foreign lands. Here are foreign lands platted & divided by streets, all seen in an hour or few minutes as you prefer. Italians & Chinese half a block apart & like the water of the Miss. & Mo. where they join yet keep apart they apparently do not intend to mix at all. Such quantities of children, all in the street, remind one of the seeds which fall from certain plants—little tiny ones running in & out of the horses' feet like rats but apparently well able to take care of themselves. Men & women & children had a Sunday look on their faces altho many stores were open & peddlers selling fruit & food like last night. What a great charity the American play ground for boys! Right in these densely settled districts where one wonders how all ever get into the houses at once, one finds these grounds where these bits of humanity have trapezes & every kind of gymnastic apparatus & ball grounds & play grounds & places for mothers & their little ones to sit in the open air & near by baths are free & to be had in the river. I forgot to tell you I saw American flags every where last night. Some men used them for cravats & women for hankerchiefs.

VI

THE CITY

The city was as irresistible for native as for foreign-born Americans. Economically, socially, and culturally more attractive than the country, the city nevertheless had problems that neither the Gilded Age nor our own age has solved. Rapid growth made these problems particularly acute. Chicago quintupled in population between 1870 and 1900, Cleveland quadrupled, and New York doubled. Phenomenal growth created fantastic congestion, inadequate water and sewer systems, unpaved and filthy streets, and an abnormally high death rate. Cheap rapid transit, designed to relieve congestion, merely furthered urban growth and tempted unscrupulous businessmen to bribe politicians for franchises. The city sheltered not only graft and corruption among its leaders but also the vice and crime of humbler citizens. Dangerous, ugly, filthy, and corrupt yet possessing beautiful residences, sections, and parks, imposing facilities, and zealous reforming citizens, the city despite its problems was exciting, fascinating, vigorous, and promising.

[40.] *"Women Are Even More Susceptible*
to This Townward Drift than Men"

Frederick Law Olmsted, pioneer urban landscape architect, explains the attraction of the city. [Frederick L. Olmsted, "Public Parks and the Enlargement of Towns," *Journal of Social Science* . . . , No. III (1871), 1-3, 5-6.]

The last "Overland Monthly" tells us that in California "only an inferior class of people can be induced to live out of towns. There is something in the country which repels men. In the city alone can they nourish the juices of life."

This of newly built and but half-equipped cities, where the people are never quite free from dread of earthquakes, and of a country in which the productions of agriculture and horticulture are more varied, and the rewards of rural enterprise larger, than in any other under civilized government! With a hundred million acres of arable and grazing land, with thousands of outcropping gold veins, with the finest forests in the world, fully half the white people live in towns, a quarter of all in one town, and this quarter pays more than half the taxes of all. "Over the mountains the miners," says Mr. Bowles, "talk of going to San Francisco as to Paradise," and the rural members of the Legislature declare that "San Francisco sucks the life out of the country."

At the same time all our great interior towns are reputed to be growing rapidly; their newspapers complain that wheat and gold fall much faster than house-rents, and especially that builders fail to meet the demand for such dwellings as are mostly sought by new-comers, who are mainly men of small means and young families, anxious to make a lodgment in the city on any terms which will give them a chance of earning a right to remain. In Chicago alone, it is said, that there are twenty thousand people seeking employment.

To this I can add, from personal observation, that if we stand, any day before noon, at the railway stations of these cities, we may notice women and girls arriving by the score, who, it will be apparent, have just run in to do a little shopping, intending to return by supper time to farms perhaps a hundred miles away.

It used to be a matter of pride with the better sort of our country people that they could raise on their own land or manufacture within their own households almost everything needed for domestic consumption. But if now you leave the rail, at whatever remote station, the very advertisements on its walls will manifest how greatly this is changed. Push out over the prairie and make your way to the house of any long-settled and prosperous farmer, and the intimacy of his family with the town will constantly appear, in dress, furniture, viands, in all the conversation. If there is a piano, they will be expecting a man from town to tune it. If the baby has outgrown its shoes, the measure is to be sent to town. If a tooth is troublesome, an appointment is to be arranged by telegraph with the dentist. The railway time-table hangs with the almanac. The housewife complains of her servants. There is no difficulty in getting them from the intelligence offices in town, such as they are; but only the poorest, who cannot find employment in the city, will come to the country, and these as soon as they have got a few dollars ahead, are crazy to get back to town. It is much the same with the men, the farmer will add; he has to run up in the morning and get some one to take "Wolf's" place. You will find, too, that one of his sons is in a lawyer's office, another at a commercial college, and his oldest daughter at an "institute," all in town. I know several girls who travel eighty miles a day to attend school in Chicago.

•   •   •

And how are things going here in Massachusetts? A correspondent of the "Springfield Republican" gave the other day an account of a visit lately made to two or three old agricultural neighborhoods, such as fifty years ago were the glory of New England. When he last knew them, their society was spoken of with pride, and the influence of not a few of their citizens was felt throughout the State, and indeed far beyond it. But as he found them now, they might almost be sung by Goldsmith. The meeting-house closed, the church dilapidated; the famous old taverns, stores, shops, mills, and offices dropping to pieces and vacant, or perhaps with a mere corner occupied by day laborers; but a third as many children as formerly to be seen in the school-houses, and of these less than half of American-born parents.

Walking through such a district last summer, my eyes were gladdened by a single house with exceptional signs of thrift in fresh paint, roofs, and fences, and newly planted door-yard trees; but happening as I passed to speak to the owner, in the second sentence of our conversation he told me that he had been slicking his place up in hopes that some city gentleman would take a fancy to it for a country seat. He was getting old, had worked hard, and felt as if the time had fully come when he was entitled to take some enjoyment of what remained to him of life by retiring to the town. Nearly all his old neighbors were gone; his children had left years ago. His town-bred granddaughters were playing croquet in the front yard.

•   •   •

. . . We all recognize that the tastes and dispositions of women are more and more potent in shaping the course of civilized progress, and we may see that women are even more susceptible to this townward drift than men. Oftimes the husband and father gives up his country occupations, taking others less attractive to him in town, out of consideration for his wife and daughters. Not long since I conveyed to a very sensible and provident man what I thought to be an offer of great preferment. I was surprised that he hesitated to accept it, until the question was referred to his wife, a bright, tidy American-born woman, who promptly said: "If I were offered a deed of the best farm that I ever saw, on condition of going back to the country to live, I would not take it. I would rather face starvation in town." She had been brought up and lived the greater part of her life in one of the most convenient and agreeable farming countries in the United States.

Is it astonishing? Compare advantages in respect simply to schools, libraries, music, and the fine arts. People of the greatest wealth can hardly command as much of these in the country as the poorest work-girl is offered here in Boston at the mere cost of a walk for a short distance over a good, firm, clean pathway, lighted at night and made interesting to her by shop fronts and the variety of people passing.

It is true the poorer work-girls make little use of these special advantages, but this simply because they are not yet educated up to them. When, however, they come from the country to town, are they not moving in the way of this education? In all probability, as is indicated by the report (in the "New York Tribune") of a recent skillful examination of the condition and habits of the poor sewing women of that city, a frantic desire to escape from the dull lives which they have seen before them in the country, a craving for recreation, especially for more companionship in yielding to playful girlish impulses, innocent in themselves, drives more young women to the town than anything else. Dr. Holmes may exaggerate the clumsiness and dreariness of New England village social parties; but go further back into the country among the outlying farms, and if you have ever had part in the working up of some of the rare occasions in which what stands for festivity is attempted, you will hardly think that the ardent desire of a young woman to escape to the town is wholly unreasonable.

[41.]   *"A Certain Old-Time Atmosphere
in the Midst
of the Prevailing Commonplaceness"*

Frederick E. Haynes describes South Boston's most popular theater. [Frederick E. Haynes, "Amusements," in *The City Wilderness: A Settlement Study . . . ,* ed. Robert A. Woods (Boston: Houghton, Mifflin and Company, 1898), pp. 176-81.]

Of all the places of amusement at the South End there was none so popular locally, and so interesting and typical in itself, as the old Grand Dime Museum, at the chief corner of the district, where Dover Street crosses Washington. As it was before the changes made in 1896, by which it became the new Grand Theatre, it introduced, or shall we say preserved, a certain old-time atmosphere in the midst of the prevailing common-placeness. The scenes presented upon its stage, the audience lost in the story enacted, seemed like bits of Dickens—incidents and characters out of those chapters in the book of life which he made so completely his own. Little imagination was needed to give to it all a reality and naturalness which has been lost in the "improvements" of the past two years. There was a certain quality in the plays to be enjoyed even by a person accustomed to higher types of amusement. The tragedy was lurid, the comedy coarse, there was much to grate upon fine sensibilities; but there was withal back of it the red blood of the simpler human feelings and passions, that made good a multitude of faults. The audiences applauded the brave lover, devoted wife, and fond mother; hissed the villain and rejoiced in his downfall. There might be absence of good taste, but there was plenty of evidence that the heart was right.

. . . Every boy and man, many of the girls, and some of the women, regard an afternoon or an evening at the Dime now and then as an indispensable part of their lives. The Dime is to them what the theatre, the opera, and the symphony are to the more fortunate classes in the community. It is the only means by which they can obtain the enjoyment that is derived from the imagination. That the craving is strong is shown by the crowded houses always to be seen at this resort.

The performance begins promptly at one o'clock with variety features. At two o'clock the drama opens. Interspersed between the acts is the "olio," consisting of a number of variety exhibits, musical, humorous, sleight-of-hand, ventriloquist, and athletic. The same performance is repeated in the evening, beginning at seven. A single play with its accompanying vaudeville features is given usually for a week; then there is a complete change of bill and frequently of actors as well. The same management has under its control two theatres in other parts of Boston, and theatres at four smaller New England cities. In 1896 it had ten stock companies and a star company. The star company, besides playing at the home houses, toured through the country.

Overwrought melodrama has all along had probably the chief popularity at the Dime, although its reign is not quite so assured as it once was. The startling situations, the portrayal of forceful human sentiments and passions, thrill the people and satisfy their demand for strong colors and broad effects. The manager says that there is now, however, more demand for frequent change in the kind of amusement. Formerly for week after week the people were content with the melodrama. They never seemed to tire of it. Now they demand an occasional society play with its pictures of a life so different from their own. Comedy, especially of the Celtic kind, has always had a prominent place in the programmes.

Many of the plays have been the standard and popular dramas that are usually no longer given in other theatres. The old favorites, like "The Two Orphans" and "East Lynne," regularly reappear at the Dime now that they have become too threadbare for the higher priced houses. The plays are touched up to suit the preferences of the people. The ghost is introduced in "Dr. Jekyll and Mr. Hyde," in order to make clear how the victim haunts the murderer. Local hits and popular "gags" are brought in. Passing incidents or well-known personalities are used as subjects of remark. All these efforts meet with ready appreciation on the part of the listeners. The nearer home such allusions come, the better they are liked; for the people, with all their love of the romantic, the sentimental, and the improbable, enjoy best of all a presentation of these features of existence with which they are familiar. The vagaries of a drunken man, the follies of an Irish servant girl, the exploits of a policeman, and other scenes from street and tenement-house life are always and everywhere hailed with loud applause. The people are at heart realists, whatever else they may be now and then. Like all the rest of us, they measure the world of the imagination by the narrow range of their own little sphere; just as did the poor woman who, on being shown the picture of a fateful scene in the French Revolution, thought it must be an eviction. The apparently morbid taste of an audience like that of the Dime for the pathetic—the family stricken with grief or distressed by want, the betrayed girl, the honest man wronged by some upstart superior—is really the natural outcome of the kind of experience with which their round of life makes them only too familiar.

In the spring of 1896 the old Grand Dime closed its doors to allow for extensive improvements. An enlarged gallery was provided for the patrons at the lowest prices. The old gallery had been the great refuge for those who had only a dime to spare for their amusement. Boys and men especially frequented it, and it has probably furnished enjoyment to more people than any similar place in Boston. It was by far the most characteristic part of the old Grand Dime. Its associations, indeed, were like those of the pit in olden times. The scene in the gallery on a Saturday or a Mon[day] night, when some thrilling melodrama or an Irish comedy held the boards, was one long to be remembered. Every seat was taken, and every inch of standing room. An experienced observer, running his eye over the gallery, could pick out the various classes of the people. The corner loafer, the out-of-work, the casual laborer, the mechanic, and the clerk were all there. The few classes unrepresented in the gallery were to be found in other parts of the house,—the cheap and flashy aristocracy in the boxes, the respectability of the district in the seats on the orchestra floor. On such a night one got at the Dime a cross-section of the population of the district.

[42.] *"Games They Always Had"*

Jacob A. Riis claims that New York City slum children "lack neither spirit nor inventiveness" in their play. "Their opportunities for mischief," however, "are greater than those for harmless amusement; made so, it has sometimes seemed . . . , with deliberate purpose to hatch the 'tough.'" [Jacob A. Riis, "The Children of the Poor," in Robert A. Woods *et al.*, *The Poor in Great Cities* (New York: Charles Scribner's Sons, 1895), pp. 114-16.]

The earliest notion of order and harmless play comes to the children through the kindergartens, to which access is now made easier every day. Without a doubt this is the longest step forward that has yet been taken in the race with poverty; for the kindergarten, in gathering in the children, is gradually but surely conquering also the street, with its power for mischief. Until it came, the street was the only escape from the tenement—a Hobson's choice, for it is hard to say which is the most corrupting. The opportunities rampant in the one were a sad commentary on the sure defilement of the other. . . . Games they always had. It is not true, as someone has said, that our poor children do not know how to play "London Bridge is falling down" with as loud a din in the streets of New York, every day, as it has fallen these hundred years and more in every British town, and the children of the Bend march "all around the mulberry bush" as gleefully as if there were a green shrub to be found within a mile of their slum. It is the slum that smudges the game too easily, and the kindergarten's work comes in helping to wipe off the smut. So far from New York children being duller at their play than those of other cities and lands, I believe the reverse to be true. They lack neither spirit nor inventiveness. I watched a crowd of them having a donkey party in the street one night, when those parties were all the rage. The donkey hung in the window of a notion store, and a knot of tenement-house children, with tails improvised from a newspaper and dragged in the gutter to make them stick, were staggering blindly across the sidewalk trying to fix them in place on the pane. They got a heap of fun out of the game, quite as much, it seemed to me, as any crowd of children could have got in a fine parlor, until the storekeeper came out with his club. Every cellar-door becomes a toboggan-slide when the children are around, unless it is hammered full of envious nails; every block a ball-ground when the policeman's back is turned, and every roof a kite-field; for that innocent amusement is also forbidden by city ordinance "below Fourteenth Street."

It is rather that their opportunities for mischief are greater than those for harmless amusement; made so, it has sometimes seemed to me, with deliberate purpose to hatch the "tough." Given idleness and the street, and he will grow without other encouragement than an occasional "fanning" of a policeman's club. And the street has to do for his playground. There is no other. Central Park is miles away. The small parks that were ordered for his benefit five years ago, exist yet only on paper. Games like kite-flying and ball-playing, forbidden but not suppressed, as happily they cannot be, become from harmless play a successful challenge of law and order that points the way to later and worse achievements. Every year the police forbid the building of election bonfires, and threaten vengeance upon those who disobey the ordinance; and every election night sees the sky made lurid by them from one end of the town to the other, with the police powerless to put them out. Year by year the boys grow bolder in their raids on property when their supply of firewood has given out, until the destruction wrought at the last election became a matter of public scandal. Stoops, wagons, and in one place a showcase containing property worth many hundreds of dollars, were fed to the flames. It has happened that an entire frame house has been carried off piecemeal and burned up on election night. The boys, organized in gangs, with the one condition of membership that all must "give in wood," store up enormous piles of fuel for months before, and though the police find and raid a good many of them, incidentally laying in supplies of kindling wood for the winter, the pile grows again in a single night as the neighborhood reluctantly contributes its ash-barrels to the cause. The germ of the gangs that terrorize whole sections of the city at intervals, and feed our courts and our jails, may, without much difficulty, be discovered in these early and rather grotesque struggles of the boys with the police.

[43.] *"Ole Man Pickett"*

Lafcadio Hearn describes the proprietor of the most popular
establishment on Cincinnati's Sausage Row, where "policemen, searching for missing property, come for information"
and "thieves searching for customers find a market." [Lafca-
dio Hearn, "Ole Man Pickett . . . ," *Cincinnati Enquirer,*
February 21, 1875, in Lafcadio Hearn, *Children of the Levee,*
ed. O. W. Frost (Lexington: The University of Kentucky
Press, 1957), pp. 54-60. Reprinted by permission of The University of Kentucky Press.]

When an exhaustive history of the Queen City comes to be written,
among the names of those who labored both for her weal and woe, few
will be more conspicuous than that of Henry Pickett, now the hero and
chief proprietor of that fashionable boulevard known as Sausage Row.
Who has not heard of "ole man" Pickett and his ranches, but who knows
what he has done for and against Cincinnati? Who has not often seen
Sausage Row in print, but who knows where it is located, and how many
human hives exist along its border? Who has not seen a record of some
criminal, or of some stolen property being found in Pickett's ranch, but
who knows what these ranches are, and what they contain? We paid
Pickett and his possessions a visit the other evening, when some seventy-
five or a hundred of the dusky frequenters of his ranches were reveling
in waltzes, polkas, lances and quadrilles. We had ample opportunity to
view the premises, and plenty of ears to hear the "ole man's" story, though
the rattling of tinware, the strains from a cracked violin, a dismal guitar
and a wheezy bass viol together with the jingling of glasses, and the calls
of "Swing partners, forward and back, first fo' right and left," were fairly
deafening to us. The premises consist of three or four saloons, eating and
dance-rooms, over which Pickett has a personal supervision. The two or
three other "cribs" or places in the row Pickett partially controls, he
being a sub-leaser. The particular ranch which we visited on the evening
in question, like all the others, is in a basement, and except on one side is
entirely underground. The bar is in the front room, and the dancing place
is located immediately in the rear. The bar-room receives a little of the
light of day, but the dance-room, save when lit by the faint flickerings of
a coal-oil lamp, is in perpetual darkness. Rafters and boards answer the

urpose of ceiling, and whitewashed stone walls are the linings on every
ide. In the extreme rear end of the dance-room the proprietor has had
artitioned off a small bed-room where he sleeps, his sleeping companion
eing his only son, a wooly-head of some ten summers, and a half-dozen
omeless curs which, out of pity, he has rescued from the street. The bar,
ance and bed-rooms altogether do not cover more than sixty-five by
wenty feet, and yet in this small space the host manages daily, and nightly
oo, to entertain from seventy to a hundred Americanized Ethiopians. A
ark skin is a necessary passport into Pickett's places. "White trash"
evelers, with one or two rare exceptions, are never admitted. A poor,
alf idiotic white girl may be seen in here occasionally, but she has been
pecially privileged because she has a negro for her "feller." In their dances
ery little order and a great deal of whisky prevails, and yet from these
ances very few disturbances have been known to arise. The average white
nan, inspired by the same kind of lightning which these black and thirsty
varriors imbibe, would only find vent for his exuberance in playfully firing
a few random shots from a well loaded revolver, or in frisking around
romiscuously with an illy proportioned bowie-knife. A mixture of brim-
tone, prussic acid, snake fangs and other harmless ingredients, makes
he white man unpleasantly demonstrative; but down on Sausage Row it
eems to make the black man submissive and even good natured. No mat-
er how drunk Pickett's guests become, over them he has very rarely lost
iis seemingly magnetic influence. The admission of white scum to his
quarters, he apprehends, would break the spell, and so he keeps it out.
He says his receptions now move off pleasantly, and so long as the colored
nan is his only patron he expects they will continue to do so.

As we entered the other evening and looked upon the three musicians
awing and picking away, the leader yelling off the changes in a low gut-
ural tone, twenty or thirty dancers on the floor shuffling around amid
rivulets of tobacco-seasoned saliva, sixty or seventy dusky faces looking
on, low-crowned hats ornamenting the heads of males, and streaming,
gorgon-like looking hair the heads of females, a pale, sickly light from the
amp shed over the scene, the sensation became weird in the extreme.

The closing of navigation on the Ohio has had a material effect on
Pickett's net receipts, inasmuch as the most of his patrons are river men.
The stoppage of work is usually a signal for these river rats to ask for
credit, as they very rarely husband any thing. Pickett never turns any
nan away from him hungry. If asked for credit he almost uniformly
gives it, and then trusts to luck and his customer's honesty for pay. During the past few weeks of cold weather this old man, who has been considered as utterly destitute of any of the milk of human kindness, has been

feeding and warming nearly a hundred destitute negroes, whom, were
not for him, the city would be obliged to support. He has fed and warme
them, too, when very little money was realized for the same. He charge
them twenty-five cents for a regular "white folks' meal at a table," te
cents for a lunch, and ten cents for the privilege of sleeping by his fir
He adheres to a European plan with a reasonable schedule of prices. H
charges, when not cashed, are entered upon a book, which the bar-tende
keeps; as Pickett himself is unable either to read or even to sign his ow
name. Henry Pickett is now over sixty-four years of age, and was bor
a slave in Goochland County, Virginia. George Pickett, an owner of ove
five hundred slaves, was his father, and a member of the Virginia Legisla
ture. His mother, an ebony black woman, was owned by a heavy plante
and slave-owner named Charles Hawchins. Hawchins had hired out som
of his chattels to George Pickett, Henry's mother among them, and that
the way Henry came about. Hawchins dying, Henry fell into the hands
his heirs, under the care of an ugly overseer. This was very galling to him
and so he took a French leave of his friends and made for the woods. H
was hunted down by bloodhounds, captured, placed in irons, lashed wit
raw-hides, rubbed down with salt and water and then set to work again
He had grown to be a perfect Titan in size, nerve and strength, and ha
come to think that slavery was not his proper element, and so he ra
away again. This time he lived for over a year in the woods, feeding upo
such fruit as he could find and such food as neighboring slaves would brin
him. With this kind of life he became tired, and so voluntarily gave him
self up to his old masters; soon had a fight with the overseer; was badl
cut up, marks of which he now bears; became a cheap "nigger" in conse
quence, and was sold. A Richmond man named James Benworth was th
purchaser. Benworth had an eye to business, and immediately offere
Pickett the privilege of buying himself for a thousand dollars' considera
tion. This was to be a legitimate freedom, and Pickett jumped at th
offer. He immediately resumed the responsibility of porter at the old Ex
change Hotel, Richmond, and began the laborious task of buying his free
dom. He had accumulated nine hundred dollars, and paid over to his mas
ter, when the original offer was reconsidered, and he was again on th
block. This time he was sold to a Mr. Thornton, and placed as a steward
on a James River packet-boat, with an understanding that if he valued hi
liberty $1,800 worth he could have it by paying for it. Thornton wa
as good as his word, finally received his $1,800, and Pickett, at the ag
of forty, was his own master for the first time. He continued with th
packet company until he had accumulated $800 more and paid over fo
his wife and child, when, in 1854, he came to Cincinnati. For the first fe

years of his life in this city he lived and worked for a sporting man on Baker street, known as Tom Curran. Having accumulated considerable, he bought a farm, saw-mill and grocery near Xenia, Greene County, where, for a time, he was prosperous, but where, after three years, he was, to use his own language, "busted up." He says he lost four or five thousand dollars in this speculation. He then came back to this city and opened a coffee-house in a cellar on Fourth street, between Main and Sycamore. The Rev. Dr. Weeds was his landlord. "Very accommodating man dat Doctor was," said Pickett; "let me sell any thing I wanted to in his ole cella." The coffee-house on Fourth street, however, did not pan out well, and so another move was made; this time to a low, dingy, dark hole on Sixth street, where he, for the first time, became notorious. His place ranked among the lowest sinks in Cincinnati. He made lots of money here, however, but being again and again hauled up by the police, his money melted away in a most mysterious manner. Again and again would he be accused of this and that crime, but through his innocence, or mayhap his lucre, he would invariably escape. Sixth street finally became too warm, too aristocratic or too something, and so he again migrated, making his final stand on Sausage Row, just east of the old Spencer House. In this place his fortune, like his whole life, has been very checkered. Here he has lost wife and children, and here he has cleared and sunk thousands of dollars. Here he has acquired the reputation of being alike the respecter of the light fingers of the prig and the strong arm of the law. Here policemen, searching for missing property, come for information, and here thieves searching for customers find a market. In the aid lent to the discovery of crime the weal of the city is here fostered, but in the encouragement given to the criminal her woe is also furthered. In the feeding and trusting of scores of colored vagrants which hang about his ranch he keeps them from the Work-house, and so contributes to the city's good by saving her a heavy expense. His colored brethren have always found him an ugly enemy and a reliable friend. The descendants of Ham, from the junction of the Allegheny to the Mississippi, know him, respect him, and fear him. Not a policeman in Cincinnati who has ever had any thing to do with Pickett will not have a good word to say for him, though at the same time they paradoxically claim him to be a bad man. Cincinnati lawyers, who have again and again helped him out of and away from some very ugly snags in the Police Court, know that he is generally prompt at paying their fees. City missionaries have found him serious, and city offenders have found him gay. Among Romans he always does as the Romans do. He is crafty and curious and frank. He is an interesting phenomenon over which the phrenological disciples of Fowler would puzzle.

Like a certain other personage occasionally heard of, when sick Pickett a saint would be, but when well a Pickett of a saint is he. He is now laid up with what he calls "busted veins," his lower limbs being constantly swollen, and he is therefore ready to converse upon death, hell, judgment, and other cheerful subjects. As an old man he can see that his days of probation are rapidly tallying. He wants to dispose of his business, but can find no purchaser. He says he wants to go to the home of his only daughter, now in Richmond, Virginia, and there die. With the expected "blues" of sickness he thinks his friends are deserting him. He fears an attack of the "King of Terrors" in Cincinnati, but believes he could meet him manfully in Richmond. In Cincinnati he believes he has been too often pushed to the wall, that in adversity all men would forsake him, and that in death he might exclaim like Logan of old, "Who is there to mourn for"—Pickett.

[44.] "The Dirtiest Wealthy City" Becomes Clean

Commissioner George E. Waring, Jr., tells how he accomplished the transformation of New York. [George E. Waring, Jr., *Street-Cleaning* . . . (New York: Doubleday & McClure Co., 1897), pp. 187, 13-14, 16, 18, 20-21, 187-89.]

The following was written in 1894 by Mr. J. S. Da Costa to a friend in Rio Janeiro:

New York seems to be the dirtiest wealthy city that I have seen. There are portions of the city that are so packed with empty vehicles of every size and shape that one is apt to think, from a view of the filthy state of all their surroundings, that after eight o'clock at night the commercial portion of the city is converted into a huge dirty public stable, unsightly and disgustingly hideous, viewed from whatever point it may be looked at.

•   •   •

Before 1895 the streets were almost universally in a filthy state. In wet weather they were covered with slime, and in dry weather the air was filled with dust. Artictial sprinkling in summer converted the dust into mud, and the drying winds changed the mud to powder. Rubbish of all kinds, garbage, and ashes lay neglected in the streets, and in the hot weather the city stank with the emanations of putrefying organic matter. It was not always possible to see the pavement, because of the dirt that covered it. One expert, a former contractor of street-cleaning, told me that West Broadway could not be cleaned, because it was so coated with grease from wagon-axles; it was really coated with slimy mud. The sewer inlets were clogged with refuse. Dirty paper was prevalent everywhere, and black rottenness was seen and smelled on every hand.

The practice of standing unharnessed trucks and wagons in the public streets was well-nigh universal in all except the main thoroughfares and the better residence districts. The Board of Health made an enumeration of vehicles so standing on Sunday, counting twenty-five thousand on a portion of one side of the city; they reached the conclusion that there were in all more than sixty thousand. These trucks not only restricted traffic and made complete street-cleaning practically impossible, but they were harbors of vice and crime. Thieves and highwaymen made them their dens, toughs caroused in them, both sexes resorted to them, and they were used for the vilest purposes, until they became, both figuratively and literally, a stench in the nostrils of the people. In the crowded districts they were a veritable nocturnal hell. Against all this the poor people were powerless to get relief. The highest city officials, after feeble attempts at removal, declared that New York was so peculiarly constructed (having no alleys through which the rear of the lots could be reached) that its commerce could not be carried on unless this privilege were given to its truckmen; in short, the removal of the trucks was "an impossibility."

. . . The condition of the streets, of the force, and of the stock was the fault of no man and of no set of men. It was the fault of the system. The department was throttled by partizan control—so throttled it could neither do good work, command its own respect and that of the public, nor maintain its material in good order. It was run as an adjunct of a political organization. In that capacity it was a marked success. It paid fat tribute; it fed thousands of voters, and it gave power and influence to hundreds of political leaders. It had this appointed function, and it performed it well.

My early acquaintance with the department was not without its amusing incidents. I found, for example, that the general superintendent had an unusual capacity for handling the roughly organized force employed in the removal of snow. He had been reported to me as a Tammany captain, and as one of the chief agencies through which his political organization had worked the department. He was strongly recommended for dismissal. Remembering the wise injunction "not to swap horses when crossing a stream," I waited until the snow season had passed. I then sent for him, and told him that he had been represented as a "rank Tammany man," etc.

He said with mild submission, "Whenever you want my resignation, it is at your service." I said, "Don't be quite so fast; let me hear your version of your case." He said, "Do you know what a Tammany man is? It is a man who votes for his job. I have been a Tammany man, and a faithful one. I have worked for the organization; I have paid regular contributions to it. But I am a Waring man now." He probably saw an unexplained smile on my face, for he said, "Don't misunderstand me. If Tammany comes into power again I shall be a Tammany man again." This frankness met its reward, and I have had the great advantage of Mr. William Robbins's active and earnest assistance from that day to this and I trust to have it for many a long day yet.

•   •   •

When the important offices had been filled attention was turned to the rank and file of the working-force. The men were assured that their future rested solely with themselves; that if they did their work faithfully and well, kept away from drink, treated citizens civilly, and tried to make themselves a credit to the department, there was no power in the city that could get them out of their places, so long as I stayed in mine. On the other hand, if they were drunkards, incompetent, blackguards, or loafers, no power could keep them in. When they found that I really meant what I said—and it took them some time to get such a strange new idea into their heads—they took on a new heart of hope, and turned their eyes to the front. From that day their improvement has been constant and most satisfactory. Their white uniforms, once so derided, have been a great help to them, and they know it; and the recognition of the people has done still more for them. Indeed, the parade of 1896 marked an era in their history. It introduced them to the prime favor of a public by which, one short year before, they had been contemned; and the public saw that these men were proud of their positions, were self-respecting, and were the object of pride on the part of their friends and relatives who clustered along their line of march.

What has really been done has been to put a man instead of a voter at the other end of the broom-handle. The "White Wings" are by no means white angels, but they are a splendid body of men, a body on which the people of New York can depend for any needed service, without regard to hours or personal comfort. A trusted sweeper, for example, will stand on a windy dock-log all night long, and night after night, protecting the city against the wiles and tricks of the snow-carters. He gets no extra pay for this, but his extra service and his hardship are compensated by the consciousness that he is doing good work, that his good work is appreciated by his officers, and that the force to which he belongs is winning public favor partly because of what he himself is doing. In other words, the whole department is actuated by a real *esprit de corps,* without which no organization of men can do its best, either in war or in peace.

• • •

New York is now thoroughly clean in every part, the empty vehicles are gone, and no such criticism as that of our Brazilian writer will ever be made again. "Clean streets" means much more than the casual observer is apt to think. It has justly been said that "cleanliness is catching," and clean streets are leading to clean hallways and staircases and cleaner living-rooms. A recent writer says:

> It is not merely justification of a theory to say that the improvement noticed in the past two and a half years in the streets of New York has led to an improvement in the interior of its tenement-houses. A sense of personal pride has been awakened in the women and children, the results of which have long been noticeable to every one engaged in philanthropic work among the tenement dwellers. When, early in the present administration, a woman in the Five Points district was heard to say to another, "Well, I don't care; my street is cleaner than yours is, anyhow," it was felt that the battle was won.

Few realize the many minor ways in which the work of the department has benefited the people at large. For example, there is far less injury from dust to clothing, to furniture, and to goods in shops; mud is not tracked from the streets on to the sidewalks, and thence into the houses; boots require far less cleaning; the wearing of overshoes has been largely abandoned; wet feet and bedraggled skirts are mainly things of the past; and children now make free use as a playground of streets which were formerly impossible to them. "Scratches," a skin disease of horses due to mud and slush, used to entail very serious cost on truckmen and liverymen. It is now almost unknown. Horses used to "pick up a nail" with alarming frequency, and this caused great loss of service, and, like scratches, made the bill of the veterinary surgeon a serious matter. There are practically no nails now to be found in the streets.

The great, the almost inestimable, beneficial effect of the work of the department is shown in the large reduction of the death-rate and in the less keenly realized but still more important reduction in the sick-rate. As compared with the average death-rate of 26.78 of 1882-94, that of 1895 was 23.10, that of 1896 was 21.52, and that of the first half of 1897 was 19.63. If this latter figure is maintained throughout the year, there will have been

fifteen thousand fewer deaths than there would have been had the average
rate of the thirteen previous years prevailed. The report of the Board of
Health for 1896, basing its calculations on diarrheal diseases in July, August, and September, in the filthiest wards, in the most crowded wards,
and in the remainder of the city, shows a very marked reduction in all, and
the largest reduction in the first two classes.

It is not maintained, of course, that this great saving of life and health is
due to street-cleaning work alone. Much is to be ascribed to improvements
of the methods of the Board of Health, and not a little to the condemnation
and destruction of rear tenements; but the Board of Health itself credits
a great share of the gain to this department.

[45.] *"Transit Facilities*
Have Improved So Slowly"

Adna F. Weber discusses New York's need of better transportation. [Adna F. Weber, "Rapid Transit and the Housing
Problem," *Municipal Affairs*, VI, No. 3 (Fall 1902), 413-14.]

Rapid Transit Necessary

The diffusion of the masses of people now herding in the barracks on
the East Side requires in the first place such transit facilities that the average workingman can reach his work without great expense either of money
or of time. The latter requirement has been fairly met in many if not most
of the smaller American cities, and even in so large a place as Boston,
while in New York transit facilities have improved so slowly that a considerable portion of the mechanic's gain from the shorter hours movement
has been swallowed up in traveling on the cars. . . .

. . . In the village or small town typical of American life before the
Civil War, a clerk, artisan or laborer would seldom spend more than 15
or 20 minutes in the morning in walking to his office or workplace; half
an hour a day would probably cover his traveling time and that was an
insignificant draft upon his leisure. But now the majority of our workers reside in cities where the distance between home and workplace is
considerable and necessitates the expenditure of an excessive amount of
time in traveling to and fro. It is unreasonable to ask the mechanic or

laborer to give up more than an hour or an hour and a half a day to this part of his work, and this means in the case of New York that the cars between the outlying cottage districts and the heart of the city must make an average speed of at least 30 miles an hour.

Cheap Transit

The other requirement mentioned was *cheap* transit. Even to the highly-paid skilled workman the five-cent fare is unduly burdensome, especially if he have a large family; to the lowly-paid day laborer or sweat-shop worker the prevailing rates are actually oppressive.

[46.] *"The Aldermen Turned a Deaf Ear"*

Milo Roy Maltbie shows how private corporations have robbed the city. [Milo Roy Maltbie, "A Century of Franchise History," *Municipal Affairs*, IV, No. 1 (March 1900), 201-202.]

. . . Who can deny that with the exception of wharves and ferries, the city does not receive an adequate return for the rights it has conferred upon private corporations? Note the many instances in which far better offers were made than finally accepted, the companies formed to speculate in franchises, and the large bribes offered. Contrast the receipts from enterprises which are run by the city—docks, ferries, waterworks—with those from franchises in private hands. Mark the dividends that are annually distributed by the various corporations, and remember that whereas the returns upon the capital actually invested are never less than the nominal dividends, they may be much larger owing to the great amount of watered stock. Study the instances in which franchises have been parted with for nothing and then, being wanted by the city, have been bought back only after paying a considerable sum. Compare the capitalized value of the payments made to the city with the value of the franchises as just assessed by the state board of tax commissioners. Take the street railroads which pay more than other undertakings, except wharves and ferries. During 1899, the city received $318,938.44 not including taxes. Suppose this were capitalized; on a three per cent basis, its value would be only $10,600,000; on a one per cent basis, $32,000,000. But the state board has estimated the franchise value at over $135,000,000, and if the board has erred in any direction, it has placed the value much too low, certainly considerably below the market value.

•   •   •

The compensation received by the city has always been very small. When the first franchises were granted, very few thought them the source of great wealth, and practically no compensation was exacted. A few far-sighted persons endeavored to persuade the council not to sell its birthright for a mess of pottage. What may be pardoned as ignorance and stupidity at first, came to be criminal negligence and downright robbery. The mayor repeatedly vetoed grants on the ground that franchises could be sold for large sums. A few members of the council time and time again voiced this fact, and offers of large compensation were frequently made by responsible persons. The aldermen turned a deaf ear.

Further, the grants were so drawn as to permit evasion, and provisions that seemed to protect public interests proved to be worthless. Witness the history of gas franchises, the fact that only two companies have paid anything to the city, and one since 1884 a paltry sum of less than $15,000 per year. Witness also the evasion in the case of electric conduits and subways. Even street railways, which alone of all franchises, except docks and ferries, pay any considerable sum, really contribute very little compared with the value of the privilege granted and the intent of the grantors. This points decidedly to one conclusion, viz., that franchises should be drawn not by the attorneys of the corporations, but by the city officials, who though harmless as doves should be wiser than serpents.

[47.] *"Corrupt to the Core"*

A police captain (Max F. Schmittberger) testifies before the State Committee Investigating the New York City Police Department. [*Report and Proceedings of the Senate Committee Appointed to Investigate the Police Department of the City of New York* (Albany: James B. Lyon, State Printer, 1895), V, 5311, 5337, 5347-50, 5362-64, 5373-74, 5378-79, 5382-83.]

Captain Max F. Schmittberger,
called as a witness on behalf of the State,
having been previously sworn, testified as follows:

Question. You are a police captain of this city?—*Answer.* Yes, sir.

Question. In command of what precinct at the present time?—*Answer.* The Nineteenth.

. . .

Question. Now, captain, at this time, in the history of your service of the police department when you became captain, was it an understood thing, and a matter of common understanding among the captains of the various precincts that they were to take advantage of any opportunity that presented itself to make money out of their respective precincts?—*Answer.* Certainly.

Question. Was that the custom universally?—*Answer.* Universally.

. . .

Question. When you went to Eighty-eighth street, how long did you remain in command of that precinct?—*Answer.* I remained there from April until the following December.

Question. What collections were made in that precinct?—*Answer.* There were some policy-shops there and some pool-rooms; that was all.

Question. How much did they pay?—*Answer.* Well, altogether about $900 a month; about $800 a month.

Question. Could you give us the number of policy-shops, because we want to be exact as we can; can you give us the number of policy-shops and the number of pool-rooms that were in that precinct?—*Answer.* I think there were about 10 policy shops and about three pool-rooms.

. . .

Question. Can you tell us how much those pool-rooms pay?—*Answer.* Two hundred dollars a month.

Question. Two hundred dollars a month each?—*Answer.* Yes, sir.

Question. Who was your wardman there?—*Answer.* Gannon.

Question. You had him transferred with you to your new precinct?—*Answer.* Yes, sir.

Question. Now, as a matter of fact, at the time of that shake up nearly all the captains transferred their wardmen with them to their new precinct, did they not?—*Answer.* The most of them.

Question. Within a very short time after the transfer of the captains?—*Answer.* Yes, sir.

Question. When you got into the new precinct of course, you told Gannon to proceed in the usual way that had been proceeded in by his predecessor from the Twenty-seventh?—*Answer.* Yes, sir.

. . .

Question. How about the liquor dealers?—*Answer.* Didn't touch them.

Question. Why did you not touch the liquor dealers?—*Answer.* Well, I didn't want to; I didn't want to have nothing to do with them.

Question. What year was that in?—*Answer.* Eighteen hundred and ninety-two.

. . .

Question. Was it not an understood thing then that the liquor dealers had made their peace with the police through Tammany Hall?—*Answer.* Yes, sir.

Question. And that instead of paying directly to the police they should pay Tammany Hall; was not that the understood thing?—*Answer.* Well, that was the understood—I don't know whether that was really so or not, that is what I heard.

Question. I am asking you for the reason for your non-interference?—*Answer.* Yes, sir.

Question. That is your reason for your non-interference?—*Answer.* Yes, sir.

. . .

Question. Now out of these $800 a month, or so that you collected in the Twenty-seventh precinct, did you give any part of that money to any police official?—*Answer.* Yes, sir.

Question. How much?—*Answer.* Twenty per cent. to Gannon and about $200 a month to Inspector Williams.

Question. Did you pursue the same method with regard to delivering that money to him every month as you had while in command of your previous precinct?—*Answer.* Same method.

Question. Went down to headquarters every month?—*Answer.* Well, sometimes he would call at the station-house and I would give it to him; sometimes I would take it to headquarters.

Question. In giving him this money, this $200 a month while you were in command in that precinct were there any words uttered at all by you and by Williams at the time that you handed this money over to him?—*Answer.* No; I would simply say, "Here is something for you," and he would take it; there would be no talk made about it.

. . .

Question. Now, what sources of revenue or collections did you find in the Twenty-second?—*Answer.* There were some policy shops there and some houses of prostitution.

Question. Disorderly-houses?—*Answer.* Yes, sir.

Question. There were some gambling-houses there, were there not?—*Answer.* They were there, but they were not doing any business; they tried to do business.

. . .

Question. Will you please tell us just how you proceeded in the Twenty-second to make the collections there?—*Answer.* Well, there was about $500 collected there a month; between $500 and $600.

Question. A month?—*Answer.* Yes, sir.

Question. From all sources?—*Answer.* Yes, sir.

Question. Policy shops?—*Answer.* Yes, sir.

Question. And disorderly-houses?—*Answer.* Yes, sir.

Question. Were there any other sources but those two?—*Answer.* That is all.

Question. I presume the policy shops paid the usual $20 a month?—*Answer.* Yes, sir.

Question. What was the average pay of the disorderly-houses?—*Answer.* Some $10, some $25, some $50.

Question. Was there any such things known there as initiation fees for opening houses?—*Answer.* Not in my time.

Question. Had you any special orders from any person regarding the protection of certain disorderly-houses, particular disorderly-houses in that precinct, apart from being there?—*Answer.* Yes, sir.

Question. Tell us what directions you had?—*Answer.* When I first went in the precinct I called upon Commissioner Martin at headquarters and he particularly mentioned some disorderly-houses in Forty-sixth street.

Question. Tell us the names of the houses, please?—*Answer.* Well, he mentioned them in general, the houses in Forty-sixth street.

Question. Was Georgiana Hastings' one of those houses?—*Answer.* No; she was in Forty-fifth street.

Question. He mentioned the houses in Forty-seventh street?—*Answer.* In Forty-sixth street.

Question. Between what blocks?—*Answer.* Between Sixth avenue and Broadway.

Question. Just give us his exact words?—*Answer.* He said, "You might leave them be there and not interfere with them until the school is built;" there was a school then in erection; "after that is built, you will have to drive them out of there;" I said, "All right;" on another occasion he telephoned for me at half-past 11 o'clock at night to be in his office the first thing in the morning; I went down there; I had received a complaint about a disorderly-house from some citizens, and I sent an officer to this house to make inquiries; that was the house 250 or 252 West Fifty-first street, Mrs. Sadie West; I sent Casey there to find out what kind of a house it was, and he rang the bell, and the woman was very reluctant to give him any information; and she asked him if he knew

Commissioner Martin; he said, "Yes;" this woman said, "Commissioner Martin is a friend of mine, and don't you do anything until you hear from him;" that same evening I received a message; that was in October some time—in September, I guess, last year.

Question. November?—*Answer.* Or November; I received a message to be at Commissioner Martin's office the next day, and he said, "Did you send an officer around to such and such a house?" giving the number; I said, "Yes, sir; the officer did it at my direction;" he said, "Well, you send that man back there and make him apologize, say he made a mistake;" I said, "Hold on, commissioner, this originates from a complaint of citizens;" "Well, I don't care; I want you to do what you are told;" so I had to send that officer back and he had to apologize, beg the woman's pardon, that he was sent there to make an investigation; I desire to correct that number; it is 234 West Fifty-first street, instead of 252.

Question. Sadie West?—*Answer.* Yes, sir.

Question. Did you receive more than one complaint from the citizens regarding that house?—*Answer.* That is all; there were several letters I received, and I sent the officer there to investigate them.

•   •   •

Question. I will ask you, before it escapes my memory, to step back with me to the Twenty-second; while in the Twenty-second did you ever hear of Georgiana Hastings?—*Answer.* Yes, sir.

Question. Was she one of the women that paid?—*Answer.* No, sir.

Question. Why did she not pay?—*Answer.* Well, she was exempt for some reason or other.

Question. That is the point I want to get at, the exemption?—*Answer.* I couldn't tell you myself.

Question. How is it that she was not assessed, and, if not paying an assessment, that she was not pulled?—*Answer.* Georgiana Hastings is a very peculiar character, and some of the gentlemen who visit her house probably would not like to see their names in print, and I presume when I went to the precinct there, that that was the reason she was never interfered with; in fact, she keeps a very quiet house, and I was given the tip, so to say, if I didn't want to burn my fingers not to have anything to do with her, and I didn't; I never saw the woman, and I wouldn't know her now if she stood before me.

Question. From what source did you get the tip?—*Answer.* I couldn't remember now; I think I got it from Captain Devery, if I remember right.

Question. He had been your predecessor?—*Answer.* No; Delaney intervened between Devery and I.

Question. I mean before Devery, he had been in that precinct?—*Answer.* Yes, sir.

Question. And he knew how the thing worked?—*Answer.* Yes, sir.

Question. Is it not a fact that you were informed that certain public officials were in the habit of visiting Georgiana Hastings' house?—*Answer.* Yes, sir.

Question. And some officials that graced the bench?—*Answer.* Yes, sir.

Question. And some officials that held commissions in the city of New York?—*Answer.* Yes, sir.

•　•　•

Question. Well, captain, we have it now that by reason of the friendly interest taken in this woman Hastings by certain public officials in this city, she was protected from interference?—*Answer.* Yes, sir.

•　•　•

Question. Now, take for instance the promotion of men; can you tell us anything about how certain men procured their promotions?—*Answer.* Yes, sir.

Question. Please tell us?—*Answer.* They paid for it.

Question. Can you give us an instance?—*Answer.* Yes, sir.

Question. Give us an instance, please?—*Answer.* Captain Martens was a patrolman in my precinct when I was a sergeant; he asked me to help him to be made a roundsman; he said he had been trying for some time and wanted to be made a roundsman; I told him he couldn't get it unless he paid for it; he asked me how much it would be; I told him I thought I could make connections with Captain Williams, that he could do it for him.

Question. Was Williams captain at the time?—*Answer.* Yes, sir; I asked Captain Williams how much it would cost to make Martens roundsman; he said, $300; he said, "You get the money and I will make him;" I got the $300 from Martens, handed it to Williams, and he was made a roundsman.

Question. After Williams said that to you, you went to Martens?—*Answer.* Yes, sir.

Question. Did Martens tell you how he got the $300?—*Answer.* No, sir.

Question. But he gave it to you in cash?—*Answer.* Yes, sir.

Question. Can you tell us the circumstances surrounding his handing you the money?—*Answer.* He gave it to me in my room in the station-house.

Question. Was that in the Nineteenth precinct?—*Answer.* In the Nineteenth.

Question. You were sergeant and he was patrolman?—*Answer.* Yes, sir.

Question. Do you remember the denomination of the bills?—*Answer.* No; I don't.

Question. How were they handed to him, in an envelope or in a roll?—*Answer.* No, sir; in a roll.

Question. What did Martens say?—*Answer.* He told me, "Here is the money."

Question. Did Martens tell you how he got the money?—*Answer.* No, sir; he didn't.

Question. How soon after you got the money from Martens did you give it to Williams?—*Answer.* The same day.

Question. On the same day?—*Answer.* Yes, sir.

Question. What did you say to Williams?—*Answer.* I told him this was Marten's money.

Question. What did he say?—*Answer.* He took it, and Martens was made a roundsman.

Question. Did Williams ever say anything to you about that after?—*Answer.* No, sir.

Question. Do you know of any other specific case?—*Answer.* Yes, sir.

Question. Tell us?—*Answer.* Martens became a candidate for sergeant; he came to me again and wanted to know how much it would cost; I told him I didn't know; I would find out; I saw again Captain Williams, asked him how much it would cost to make Martens sergeant; he said, $1,600; Martens brought me the $1,600 and I handed it to Williams; Martens was not made sergeant for quite a while, and he commenced to run to my house and bother me about this money; he said, "Here, I have given you this money a couple of months ago and there is no sign of my being made sergeant;" I said, "Now, the captain has charge of this thing; you will be made in time; have patience;" and finally he began to press me so hard for the money that I couldn't hold him any longer; he wanted to know what he was to get for the money, I told this to Williams, and Williams put on his hat and coat and went down to headquarters and Martens was made a sergeant that day.

Question. Do you know of any other cases than the two that you have testified to?—*Answer.* Well, I had a conversation with Martens about his captaincy when he was a candidate for captain; yes, he told me then it would cost him $14,000.

Question. Fourteen thousand dollars?—*Answer.* Yes.

Question. Did you have anything to do with his being made a captain? —*Answer.* No, sir.

• • •

Question. You have come here and performed an act in the service of the State, which may subject you to criticism?—*Answer.* I know it will.

Question. Possibly abuse; you understand that?—*Answer.* I know it will.

Question. But is it not a fact that owing to the developments before this committee, showing the corrupt and rotten condition of affairs in the police department, you feel justified in coming forward and stating all you know?—*Answer.* Yes, sir.

Question. For the benefit of the people of this city and of this State?— *Answer.* I feel that the pillars of the church are falling and have fallen, and I feel in justice to my wife and my children that I should do this.

Question. The pillars of the temple have fallen; when you say the pillars of the church, that is, do you mean the structure of the police department?—*Answer.* Yes, sir.

Question. You feel that the whole structure has been exposed to such an extent, and its inner rottenness and corruption so exposed, that you are justified in coming forward and stating your participation?—*Answer.* Yes, sir.

Question. Now, captain, you have found in your long years of service, 22 years of service, that the police department of the city of New York has grown to be corrupt to the core; is it not a fact?—*Answer.* Yes, sir.

• • •

Question. Is there any recognition of merit at all in the department as now conducted, apart from money considerations or political influence?— *Answer.* To a very small extent; it is either politics or money.

Question. So it makes no difference how good an ordinary policeman performs his duty, or how excellent his record, there is no promotion for him?—*Answer.* There is in exceptional cases; where, for instance, a man committed some very meritorious act which would call upon him the attention of the public, where the commissioners would take action probably and promote him.

Question. But as a general rule he must either have political influence or money considerations?—*Answer.* That is generally the case.

Question. That has a very demoralizing influence on the efficiency of the force, has it not?—*Answer.* The rank and file are all right if only properly handled.

• • •

Question. The condition of affairs which has been sworn to by you touching the bribery and corruption in the police department, does it pervade the whole department?—*Answer.* I want to say one thing in favor of Superintendent Byrnes; I really think that Superintendent Byrnes is an honest and fair man, and intends to do what is right, if he were really not hampered, and allowed to do what he wants to do; I think this is the secret of the whole trouble.

Question. Outside of this one man that you exempt, can you say that outside of this one man, that the system itself is corrupt?—*Answer.* It is, to the core.

[48.] *"The Committee Put On Its Spectacles"*

The House Postal Committee investigates "obscene literature and articles of immoral use." [*National Republican* (Washington), February 4, 1876, p. 1.]

Anthony Comstock, secretary and special agent of the New York society for the suppression of vice, had a hearing before the House Postal Committee yesterday, in advocacy of a bill for the suppression of trade in and circulation of obscene literature and articles of immoral use. The bill before the committee on the subject more definitely defines the punishment of offenders than the act of Congress approved March 3, 1873. Mr. Comstock had with him for exhibition a large lot of the worst specimens of pictures and appliances for the induction and cultivation of vicious practices that could be imagined by the basest mind. The committee put on its spectacles and investigated them with fear and trembling, as well it might, for really the ingenuity displayed in efforts to demoralize the youth of this country surpasses credibility.

[49.] *"You Will Meet Opium-Slaves by the Score"*

Lafcadio Hearn suggests that temperance leaders might better have "labored and agonized . . . with the druggists and opium dealers of our country" than to have demolished "demijohns, wine casks and beer barrels." [Lafcadio Hearn, "Opium and Morphia . . . ," *Cincinnati Enquirer,* March 14, 1875, p. 2.]

Had those mothers and maidens in Israel who stalked up and down the thoroughfares, villages and cities of Ohio last spring, testing, as it were, the efficacy of prayer, invoking God's help in demolishing demijohns, wine casks and beer barrels, and in exorcising spirits generally, the spirit of enterprise included—had they, we say, known or cared any thing about the terrible opium thralldom which, without resistance, is annually gathering in its thousands of victims, they would have been quite apt to have labored and agonized not a little with the druggists and opium dealers of our country; they would have made some frail and futile efforts to break the chains which are being forged in almost every household throughout the land; they perhaps would have offered battle, and at the same time sung psalms to the great, brown dragon which is slowly settling down upon America, and gorging itself with victims.

The increase in the quantity of opium and its kindred poisons consumed in the United States alone is alarming, and should startle every well-meaning citizen—should arouse the attention of law-observers and law-makers. Walk along the streets of this city any day, and you will meet opium-slaves by the score. Whether with or without their subtile drug, you can scarcely fail to recognize them. If under its potent influence, you will notice their faded and shining skin, and a strange, basilisk glitter to their eye. If without this fearful, poisonous stimulant, you can see their repulsive, leathery complexion, their sunken and expressionless eye, and their languid and uncertain steps. They are slaves, abject slaves, suffering exquisite tortures, and not a street of Cincinnati is without them. They are not living—they are simply existing, and their days are made up of spasmodic fits of desperation. To them the pale horse and rider are generally welcome visitors, and over their unnatural deaths the mummery of an inquest is seldom known. Once in the fetters of opium or morphia, they are, with very rare exceptions, fettered for life. An incubus is upon them. They are held down with the strength of a Titan, and resurrection is foreign to all probability.

The last statistics show that there are now being imported into this country alone from Smyrna, India and China, the enormous amount of twenty-one thousand pounds of opium annually, and the stock in New York to-day consists of five hundred cases, of one hundred and fifty pounds each. Messrs. Powers & Weightman, of Philadelphia, the sole manufacturers of morphia, report that the demand for that poison is greater than the supply, and that, being sold ahead, they can take no orders for immediate delivery.

The price of opium in 1871 was but $3 87½ per pound; now with an increased quantity on hand, the price has reached $7 75, in gold. To be sure, great quantities of this terrible drug go into medicines, and for that one reason the demand has been increased. Hypodermic injections are becoming a convenient and popular mode of treatment on the part of physicians, and they, therefore, demand a larger supply. Chemists have found it one of their convenient agents, and they, too, call more loudly for its importation. But it is not the legitimate consumption which has so greatly increased the demand. Wholesale druggists are a unit in the belief that its illicit consumption is growing month by month, and retail druggists will tell you that they know this to be the case. . . . One wholesale druggist of Cincinnati alone disposes of 1,000 pounds of opium and 1,600 ounces of morphine every year. Like sugar and calicoes, these poisons have become staple, and on them, therefore, the wholesale dealers make no money. They sell because of their customers' demand. They would gladly banish the whole trade, and they would be the first to advocate a law preventing its use for other than medicinal purposes.

Its consumption is a disease, and it prevails among mechanical, business and professional men, and is especially prevalent among those of the weaker sex. In Cincinnati, victims to this terrible and poisonous appetite are known to daily grovel under its influences, victims occupying high and respected positions in society. Many of them have been slowly drawn into an opium-eating habit through the wiles of narcotic medicines. More have cultivated a taste and demand for its strange influences, have voluntarily drawn the chains about them, have with their eyes open become entangled in its strangling coils. Some have taken in the juice of the poppy to relieve pain; others, knowing the consequence, but urged on by a fascination for the horrible, have begun its use, and sought to break off when it was too late. Slaves to this appetite are found in the most orthodox of churches, and ministers have been known to draw inspiration from its subtle power. Who in Cincinnati has not heard of a prominent Ohio clergyman, who, some three or four years since, in one of our rural towns, hanged himself while his congregation was expectantly waiting his appearance in church? Whoever knew, however, that his suicide was caused by the tortures opium had inflicted? A slave for years, and eloquent only when opium pervaded every vein and artery of his system, he resolved to become disenthralled, to shake off his chains and be once more a man. In the absence of his stimulant, consistent with opium's influence, he beheld a perfect apocalypse of horror. He knew he could not face his congregation while in such a nightmare, and he knew that he could only find relief in his accustomed poison or in an entrance to the shadowy world. Firmly set against relief in the former course he deliberately chose the latter.

In the lower walks of life opium slaves are counted by the hundred. In the brothels opium reigns supreme. The writer was informed by a prominent retail druggist that he daily refused opium, morphia, or laudanum to scores of Cincinnati's *demi-mondes*. They possibly seek forgetfulness, and what agent could better answer their purposes? They can produce an intellectual torpor or ethereal bliss by its power. What wonder that when for a moment left alone, when recollections possibly of an innocent childhood come thronging on, when gloom and terror seem to be settling down, when nightly spectacles are floating in the air, what wonder, we say, that these "unfortunates" do resort to this potent drug, and in its wild delirium dream dreams of dazzling light, of unutterable splendor, of Monte Cristo wealth and luxury? What wonder that they become slaves to its influence when ambition is all gone and no motives for moral effort exist?

Men seek to drown their sorrow in this poison as drunkards do in rum. When once slaves to its power, without its influence they are known to writhe in tortures. But under its spell from anguish they are transformed to a state of mythological bliss. The insignificant becomes magnificent, ugliness becomes transcendently beautiful, and from measuring the depths of despair they experience the ecstatic raptures of the blest. They revel, as it were, among the vapors of death. But these slaves experience such wonderful extremes that change even becomes monotonous: Desperation becomes their constant attendant, and recklessness is their only guide. The quantities of poison which they consume are fabulous, and hard to be believed. One Cincinnatian known to the writer daily takes from twenty-five to thirty grains of morphia, or over a hundred times what would constitute a powerful dose in a desperate case of sickness. Not long since a morphia-eater, made prematurely old, shrunken and shriveled into the proportions of an Egyptian mummy, applied for admission into the Cincinnati Hospital, who consumed the fabulous dose of sixty grains a day. The abject servitude in which an opium-eater exists is a hundred-fold more to be dreaded than that of the alcoholic slave. The latter can sometimes reform; the former almost never. Reformed opium-eaters are exceedingly rare. Cincinnati is only known to possess one, and he only recovered from his opium by resorting to the bondage of another powerful stimulating agent. The slaves to this drug are never brutal like slaves to rum, but they are bound tighter; they are held with a firmer grasp. Once well in its quick-sands and only efforts most superhuman can save them from the prompt and certain hospitality of a grave-yard sexton.

[50.] *"I Will Take the Visions on Trust!"*

In a letter to his novelist brother, William James describes his "trip." [William James to Henry James, Chocorua, June 11, 1896, in *The Letters of William James*, edited by his son Henry James (Boston: The Atlantic Monthly Press, 1920), II, 37. © 1920 by Henry James, renewed 1948 by William James and Margaret James Porter. Reprinted by permission of Paul R. Reynolds, Inc.]

. . . I had two days spoiled by a psychological experiment with *mescal,* an intoxicant used by some of our Southwestern Indians in their religious ceremonies, a sort of cactus bud, of which the U. S. Government had distributed a supply to certain medical men, including Weir Mitchell, who sent me some to try. He had himself been "in fairyland." It gives the most glorious visions of color—every object thought of appears in a jeweled splendor unknown to the natural world. It disturbs the stomach somewhat, but that, according to W. M., was a cheap price, etc. I took one bud three days ago, was violently sick for 24 hours, and had no other symptom whatever except that and the *Katzenjammer* [hangover] the following day. I will take the visions on trust!

VII

EDUCATION

The vast majority of Gilded Age Americans received a grade school education. Although illiteracy dropped from 20 per cent in 1870 to 11 per cent in 1900, it was much higher among non-whites (80 per cent in 1870 and 45 per cent in 1900). Even though John Dewey's "progressive" ideas were enunciated by 1900, virtually all schools stressed "the three R's," rote memory, and harsh discipline. Beyond grade schools there were some urban high schools, and self-education in city libraries, museums, and lecture halls was possible.

Higher education was vastly different in the Gilded Age than it is today. Participation was limited to the fortunate few. Narrowly prescribed curriculums and rigid social regulations contrast with the widespread choice of studies and freedom on today's campuses. Nevertheless, during the Gilded Age higher education underwent profound changes. From 1870 to 1900 college graduates tripled while the total population doubled, the elective system was introduced, the domination of the clergy was broken, and, with the rise of graduate education, universities became centers of research as well as centers of education.

[51.] *"What the State Refuses to Pay for Education It Gladly Pays for Penitentiaries"*

T. Thomas Fortune describes to a Senate Committee conditions in the South and pleads for federal aid. [Senate Committee on Education and Labor, *The Relations Between Labor and Capital* . . . (Washington, D. C.: United States Government Printing Office, 1885), II, 524-25, 533.]

Aside from the vastly inadequate work being done in the South by the States, it should not be omitted here that Northern churches and organizations and individuals contribute annually to the education of the freedmen quite as much as the States; but the contributions from these sources are uncertain and fluctuating. Yet, after all that is done is considered, it must be conceded that ignorance is growing in the South as rank as the weeds that choke her corn and cotton. Whether it be the poverty of the people of the States, or disinclination of the people to tax themselves for the rooting out of illiteracy and the vices it breeds, I am not prepared to say; but that the evil is vast and menacing, all must concede. The rural journals of the South, which are usually ignorant of the first principles of political economy, object to popular education, on the ground that the blacks pay no taxes, supremely oblivious that the laboring classes of every country always create capital, and pay in rental the taxes of the land-owner, who has no more inherent right in ownership of the soil than the laborer. What the State refuses to pay for education it gladly pays for penitentiaries, preferring a pound of remedy to an ounce of cure.

It must not be forgotten that the teachers employed in the South labor under many disadvantages, which react with fearful effect upon the pupils. Because of the miserable compensation and the shortness of the school term, together with social isolation and political intolerance of the South, competent teachers cannot and are not always secured. The school term in the South does not average more than four months of the year, and I doubt much if the salaries paid will average $30 per month, subject to further reduction on school warrants by regular scalpers, merchants, and others. At least, such was my unfortunate experience in Florida as a teacher. And, then, these school teachers are subjected to every species of persecution from school superintendents, trustees, and the white braggarts of the town. The position of a colored school teacher in the South is not a desirable one from any standpoint. Before I would teach again in the South I would drive a dray on the streets.

I do not believe in centralization of government. I know the evils which come upon the people by merging into the hands of the few men, who must of necessity administer government, more power than they should control, and yet I am thoroughly convinced that the education of the people is a legitimate function of government—not in any sense a measure of centralization, but eminently one of self-preservation. We make lavish appropriations for harbors, forts, the Navy, and the Army, for the common defense, but illiteracy is a far more insidious foe from within than any that can or will assail us from without.

•   •   •

Question. I understand you to say that this matter of education is one involving not only colored people, but white people?—*Answer.* Yes; I rode through the county of Madison once, on a mule, and I did not come across a school house from the time I left until I got to Madison.

Question. How far was that?—*Answer.* Eighteen miles. I passed by, say, twenty houses, occupied by poor whites, during that time. The fact is, the poor whites in the backwoods of Florida are getting very little or no education. Each decade you will find negro illiteracy being cut down much more rapidly than white illiteracy, because these poor white people have always stood back, and do not improve any more now than they did twenty years or forty years ago. They have a mule and a cow, and own twenty acres of "piney" woods, and they never get any higher than that, as a general thing. They live in a clayey country, and a good many of them eat clay.

Question. What do you mean by eating clay?—*Answer.* I mean that they live in the "piney" woods in the clay country, and have a reputation for eating clay when they are young. They certainly have a very clayey aspect, even in their old age. In the New York Sun, a few months ago, I saw an article on the same subject of clay-eating.

[52.] *"The College Tried to Ban Switches"*

Julia B. Foraker relives her college days at "old Delaware" (now Ohio Wesleyan University). [Julia B. Foraker, *I Would Live It Again: Memories of a Vivid Life* (New York: Harper & Brothers Publishers [now Harper & Row, Publishers, Inc.], 1932), pp. 55-64. © 1932 by Julia B. Foraker, renewed 1960 by Florence M. Foraker Matthews. Reprinted by permission of the publisher.]

It was quite against the design of the founders of old Delaware that "the sexes," students-under-the-elms, should meet. Boys and girls did not come there to meet each other. (Ah, but didn't they . . . !) A rule existed that forbade "females" to look at, speak to, write to, even dream of the university "men"—except on Saturday night from eight to nine sharp. That was reception night. Gentlemen might call. One hour! Girls who had no beaux to receive hung over the bannister—"reception door must always be left open"—and jeered with mischievous eyes. Mrs. Donelson, governess of the college, received with us during the whole of those racing sixty minutes. When nine o'clock struck her hand was already on a bell—irreverently, the "cow bell"; she rang it sharply. This meant, and we knew it, "All ashore that's going ashore"; in other words, the gentlemen were to leave. But it was much harder to get them to go than it was to get them to come. It ended by dismissing the girls to their rooms first, then dowsing the gas. There was nothing else left for our beaux to do but to go home.

And yet, how romance thrived in that old town! I think it was the famous sulphur spring on the campus that betrayed the authorities. It is uphill work trying to keep down romance when there is a spring to furnish an excuse for a short walk at any time. The waters, so pure, so healthful—and so dangerous! In spite of the Puritan fiat, President Rutherford B. Hayes managed to meet and become engaged to Lucy Webb at Delaware; Vice-President Charles Warren Fairbanks met his wife, Cornelia Cole, there; many other names which the public came to know figured in those Delaware matches.

As I look back upon it I think that life in that fresh-water college of the 'sixties was as quaint and wonderful as anything that ever was. . . .

• • •

. . . Social occasions at Delaware were so jealously conceded that each one had a thrill beyond anything thereafter. Taboos were on all worldly amusements. There was to be no dancing; above all, there was to be no *waltzing*. "Huggin' up," our preacher called it, "two strangers huggin' up." There were no cards, no play-goings, no rope at all as we understand it for our boys and girls today. I remember that one of the divinity students was expelled in his senior year for attending a performance of "The Merchant of Venice." The adventure took him to Columbus and made him miss chapel the next morning. One of the old presidents, Doctor McCabe, held that a student must be in chapel unless dead. Foraker told me later that a roommate of his, troubled by the severe sentence on the man who saw Shylock, disposed of at a great sacrifice a ticket he had secretly purchased for Charlotte Cushman as Lady Macbeth. Another classmate was pitched out of the Methodist Church for attending a small town dance—he was eighteen at the time; the worst of it was that the boy never again entered a church. The next thing we heard of him was terrible—he was reading Tom Paine's *Age of Reason*.

Far more dramatic, more emotional than the theater of that day were the midwinter revivals. Church-college towns were swayed by them, and some of the great revivalists whom I remember had certainly, though their sincerity could not be questioned, the gifts of very moving actors. Always they drew crowds.

But do not imagine that fun with a rare edge did not flourish then quite "as if life held no tomb"—after Lord Byron's hint. Roastin'-ear parties when the woods were like flame and the air was like ice-cold new cider. Unearthly sleigh rides. Snow was snow then; often the driver had to set up a stake to see where in the drifts he was going. Not that we sleigh-riders cared! And lectures—we went not to be improved, but to see each other, of course! The shallow, sensational "lyceum lectures" were the rage immediately after the Civil War. Anybody who for any reason had become notorious through the newspapers was hired to lecture; a man who had been in state's prison for felony, and was now in the legislature, lectured. A woman who had been captured and outraged by the Ute Indians *lectured.*

Of the great speakers, I heard Dickens at Delaware during his second and last visit to America in 1868. I cannot think that anyone ever heard a person read with such inimitable realism and charm as this "foreigner" (they called him that) in a black velveteen jacket. I remember the jacket and the charm, but of what the author read only the unforgetable death of Little Nell, which provoked sobs. Anna Dickinson, who had written a shocking, immensely-read book with a black-and-white theme, appeared in ashes-of-roses cashmere with a long train, lectured on Joan of Arc, and created a havoc in hearts. What was a *pretty* woman like that doing in politics? And Bret Harte, the literary idol of muslin maidens, enchanted us. I think we went expecting to see a handsome "Jack Folinsbee" or a "Jack Hamlin" type, coolly insolent and fascinating. But Bret Harte had a scholar's quiet voice, poet's hair, a little long and parted in the middle, and wasn't it very gray? and young, dark eyes, brilliant almost as if with fever. He talked about the "Argonauts of '49"—and you could have heard a pin drop.

Everything was done—same old care—to make forbidden fruit tempting. We had no sports except croquet. There was, probably still is, a millpond where a fallen tree had created a dangerous current. It was put out-of-bounds. Worse than dangerous, swimming was unladylike. After that the millpond became secretly and immensely the rage. The brightest girl in school (she had promised, after repeated offenses, that she would never go to the pond again) was drowned there; a girl with her was miraculously brought back. The two had clutched at each other's long hair, were wound and bound in it. I find in my journal of '66 reference to a rumor that "the room above the Olentangy engine-house was to be turned into a gymnasium for the men." I don't remember any talk of athletics for us girls. What would we have done with sports in our tight stays, our crinolines, our preoccupation with "the crimp"—our "switches"?

The college tried to ban switches. They might as well have tried to
ban the leaves from coming out on the trees. It was the height of the
woman's-crowning-glory-her-hair ideal, hers or someone else's, it didn't
matter. I did not wear a switch, but it was only because I had more hair
than I knew what to do with, anyway. No woman under ninety-five was
free from hair vanity. One day my history teacher, Miss Brown, thin,
prim, and forty, sent word that she wished to see me in her classroom
at a certain hour. Very ominous. Now what had I done? Miss Brown
looked forbidding as I entered the room; she asked me to close the door,
then, guardedly—would I lend her my switch for next reception night?
I was so relieved, I could have given her my hair! The switch craze
must have reached its height about 1873, when one phase of the panic
of that year was expressed in advertisements of a "Crisis in Human
Hair." Shop windows dangled with bargains.

Our graduation exercises were Spartan endurance tests for the audience. I have before me the "Order of Exercises" of that hot June 24,
1868. The program began at half-past eight in the morning and went
on all day long. Every girl in the class of twenty-one read an essay. Interspersed were prayers and musical numbers, mostly polkas for four hands.
The subject of the last essay on that day was "Who Are Waiting for
Us?" The question fell on ears jaded by the reflections of sweet girl
graduates for eight solid hours. And it was supper-time. I'm afraid that
the number of those waiting for us was a little thin.

•   •   •

One event of Delaware days I shall remember forever. It was the
night of an entertainment given by our dramatic club. The program
depicted our country during the Civil War. A girl who represented the
South was dressed in black and had chains hanging from her wrists. I was
the North. I wore white and on my head a crown in red, white, and blue
paper after the shield of the United States. I should not have remembered
the occasion and the parts we played but for the fact that the next day the
news came that President Lincoln had been assassinated. Our chapel
was a small frame building with a bell in the tower. The bell was rung by
hand. That day, April 15, 1865, the bell tolled all day long. We girls took
turns at the rope. I remember pulling it until my hands were blistered.

Later, when Lincoln's funeral train went through the country on the
way to Illinois, it stopped at all the places at which the President's train
had stopped when he was on his way to his first inauguration. One of
these towns was Columbus, twenty-five miles from Delaware. I went there,
irresistibly moved, like thousands of others, to pay a last respect. The
coffin was placed on a catafalque under the great dome of the State House,

which at that time had entrances from the north, south, east, and west. The procession was formed four abreast and came from High Street, which is south of the Capitol. The lines passed through the door and divided at the bier, two going out of the eastern and two out of the western door. I do not recall that anyone I knew was with me. I only remember passing through and looking down at Lincoln's white face.

VIII

POLITICS

The Republican party dominated Gilded Age politics. Its strength lay in the North and the West with support rooted more in the Civil War than in contemporary issues. The minority Democratic party combined urban, wet, immigrant, Catholic machines with the rural, dry, Anglo-Saxon, Protestant South. By voting Democratic, the immigrant struck a blow against the pre-Civil War Nativists and the Southerner against his Civil War adversaries, the "Black" Republicans.

Despite intense political partisanship, the two major parties were never more alike than in the 1870s and 1880s. Until 1896 neither party challenged the dominant forces in American society, though both parties had dissenters. Democratic dissenters, however, differed from Republican dissenters. Many Republicans objected bitterly when their party abandoned the Negro after 1877 when his vote was no longer needed, while the Democratic party was consistently hostile to the Negro. Though most professional politicians were against civil service reform, the Republican rank and file supported it more heartily than did Democrats. More Democrats than Republicans favored a downward revision of the tariff and the free coinage of silver.

Rocked by the Panic of 1893, Democrats espoused the free silver views of the agrarian Populists, challenged the established order and in 1896 suffered a resounding defeat which strengthened the Republican party in urban areas. Subsequent Democratic opposition to imperialism merely confirmed that party's minority status. Though many distinguished Republicans also attacked imperialism, the dominant mood of that party and of the country at the close of the Gilded Age was imperialistic.

THE POLITICIANS

[53.] *"Where the Real Contest Occurs"*

A political observer working in Boston's South End describes
the political boss, the ward heeler, and the caucus. (The
author of this selection withheld his name "out of consideration for certain interests that involve outside persons.")
["The Roots of Political Power," in *The City Wilderness:
A Settlement Study . . . ,* ed. Robert A. Woods (Boston:
Houghton, Mifflin and Company, 1898), pp. 125-30, 139-40,
143-47.]

The boss has reduced to a science the knack of dominating men. If a
"jolly" or the "glad hand" will not carry his point, he can quickly frown.
The frown of the boss is supposed to carry terror to the hearts of those to
whom he has rendered favors, or who expect jobs. This is easily accounted
for, as without his approval no one in the ward can get a City job.

On the whole, partly for the love of position and power, and partly from
a good heart, the boss enjoys doing good turns for men. Stories are told by
his admirers of his generous deeds. For instance, he has been known to
pay the funeral expenses of poor people who have no insurance. At Christ-
mas time and Thanksgiving he gives turkeys to certain needy families.
Dance tickets, baseball passes, tickets to the theatre, railway passes, and
so forth,—which cost him nothing, being simply incidental results of his
tools in the common council or the legislature voting "right,"—are distributed with wise discrimination. He is always ready to treat. Some go so
far as to say that if he died to-morrow his friends would have to pay his
funeral expenses. This all sounds very generous; but the chief admirers of
the boss cannot deny that when the supremacy in the ward is at all en-
dangered, he makes capital of all his good deeds. In other words, every
man to whom he has granted a favor is made to feel that the boss expects
a vote.

I do not see how any man in his position, however good his character to
begin with, could do otherwise than use men as checkers on a board. His
ambition to boss the party in his ward necessitates his looking upon men
continually from the point of view of votes. The logic of the boss system
demands this. Votes are his business,—they mean money, power. The

boss can never be a disinterested member of society. He is forced to make
men act and vote with him,—the weaker their wills, the fewer their convictions, the better for him. He gives another drink to the drunkard: he
has a vote. The only morality he seeks in men is loyalty to him. The merit
system he regards always with a horror and indignation which would be
amusing if it were not so serious.

•   •   •

The boss is always strictly orthodox in his politics; he is intensely
partisan. Independency is the unpardonable sin in his eyes. He grows really
eloquent over "party harmony;" he storms and raves, he plots, he pleads,
for party harmony. He is really in earnest. His constituency like this
loyalty of his, too. He deceives them. Sometimes he deceives himself. He
always knows, however, that party harmony brings greater party success,
more patronage, larger favors from corporations. Party harmony does not
mean to the boss the greater ascendency of party principles; it stands to
him for good business, greater returns.

•   •   •

There are certain lesser figures characteristic of ward politics known
as "heelers." They do the dirty work. As a rule, they prefer to serve the
well-established boss, as he can best protect them if they are found out
and prosecuted in the execution of their villainy. As a rule, a "heeler" is a
broken-down "bum," afraid of work, fond of his cups, in touch with loafers
and the semi-criminal class, more of a fox than they, energetic enough in
a campaign, possessed of a strong dramatic sense, loving the excitement
of ward politics with its dark plots and wire pulling, glad to be lifted into
temporary importance by having money to spend on the "boys."

Some personal touches may make the heeler a little more real. One
whom I know wears eye-glasses, which are in picturesque contrast to the
unshaven face, filthy white shirt partly hidden by a frayed necktie, and
more filthy clothes sadly in need of repair. Once, on the eve of election,—
when therefore he had some money in his pocket,—I remember he had on
a clean collar and a new tie, but the shirt was still dirty. Perhaps his ambition stopped short of a clean shirt—it meant just so much drink. He lives
with a "policy writer" and occasionally helps him in his work. In reality a
bar-room loafer, he knows the semi-criminal class and "bums" better than
any one else in the ward. He is just as fond of loafing as the idlest one
of the lot. Consequently he is known to them as "their kind," but his intelligence and "gift of the gab" make him a leader. He has a "frog in the
throat" voice, which becomes barely a croak by caucus night. His method
of buttonholing and poking out his head at a man, in very earnestness, is
well calculated to be convincing. He really has considerable managing

bility; and if he were clean for once and had a new suit, you might easily place him as a factory manager or a captain in a regiment.

•   •   •

In nearly all tenement-house wards, one party is strongly in the majority. Such being the case, a nomination at the caucus usually means an election at the polls. The caucus is therefore the place where the real contest occurs. There is no single event in the ward that can equal the caucus for interest. It is a scene where the various gangs meet, as so many tribes, and fight for supremacy; where ambitious young men strive together for a "start" in life; where fortunes are made and lost; where sensational attempts are made to "down" the boss; it is a scene where a strong, rough, "jollying" personality tells as in the good old days of the fighting barons. Again, it is a busy mart where men are bought and sold, a place where the drunkard can get the price of another drink, a place full of surprises, of unsuspected combinations, of damaging circulars sprung too late for answer, of small leaders fighting under new banners. It is besides the great social event for the men of the ward, when they gather in crowds and push and jostle and "jolly" and joke, and yell for their favorite, and bet on him as they might bet on horses. It is, moreover, a leveling event; an event in which the "thug" feels, not as good, but better than his more respectable neighbor. Finally the caucus is a place of action. It is the great ward drama —full of strong human touches, too often potent in tragedy to free institutions and the common welfare.

•   •   •

The caucus is the scene where all this network of social life and these various typical characters in ward politics come fully into play. On entering the caucus room at 7 P. M., one would see a line stretching on two sides of the great hall and reaching into the street. Men fill the hall and the yard. All along the line are the various lieutenants of the different candidates peddling the tickets of their favorites. The candidates themselves usually stand in line where they can speak to their friends and give them the "glad hand." All is noise and action. Men push each other along the line in good-natured rough fashion. The ticket peddlers poke their cards into each successive face from the gate to the rail, and loudly call the names of their patrons. As the evening wears on, curious yells are given for the popular candidates, answered by cat-calls from the friends of their opponents. Perhaps a rough, jolly gang will throw up some fellow into the air, and as he comes down knock his hat in. Occasionally the disputes of rival heelers will issue in a fight. All around, one will see a fine assortment of "bums" going from candidate to candidate and quietly "touching" them for a half dollar, a quarter, or even the price of a drink. To refuse is to be called a "hinge,"—and stinginess is the most unpopular sin in the ward. Young men with ball tickets, benefit tickets, and other such things to sell will also go from candidate to candidate. To refuse to buy is dangerous. "Touching" is an art of which a caucus produces many devotees.

Heelers may be seen passing out to a neighboring saloon with a group of men, and sending them back to vote "right;" perhaps giving them tickets and a name to vote upon. There are many men who never attend a caucus. Their names repeaters can use with little fear of detection. Frequently the right of a repeater to vote is loudly challenged by the opponents of the machine. Then there is an excited rush to the rail. As a rule, the warden, all powerful, only turns his back, or smiles sardonically.

In this boisterous crowd the boss walks as a petty sovereign. In close contests he has, of course, all the machinery described, social and political, in good working order. He is there now to put into execution plans already made, and to meet "emergencies." Occasionally he stands near the entrance of the booths scanning each passing voter, smiling and chatty, or scowling and gruff, always masterful, hypnotizing many men into doing his bidding when they had otherwise made up their minds. In meeting candidates opposing those of his choice, he jokes with them or looks at them witheringly, as serves his purpose. If his opponent has brought out a new worker, he usually seeks an introduction, smiling and affable. Occasionally in a close contest he calls some effective worker of his opponent aside and makes him a tempting offer, provided he will get "suddenly sick" and drop out of the game. Such an offer is carefully adapted to suit the case in hand. The boss tries to keep posted on the "wants" of each man. It is important information in the complications of ward politics.

In the course of the evening a repeater may be arrested. As the man is hurried out of the place, a great crowd following, the lieutenant of the boss runs to the police station to "make it all right," or to go bail. In the mean time, the boss finds the "informer," and before an admiring and much impressed crowd denounces him for "swearing away a man's liberty." His tones are so dramatic, so earnest, so morally indignant, that faces quite unused to seriousness look ludicrously grave and convinced. It is pure buncombe, but the boss knows his audience; he gains many votes to compensate for his slight loss.

If it happen to be a caucus in which the opposition grows stronger and stronger, he may be seen darting here and there holding excited conversations with some local leader or with one of his own workers, or perhaps sending some heeler to secure more voters or engage a noted repeater. "Bums," the semi-criminal class, his own immediate and more respectable followers, are all in the caucus room ready to be manipulated at any such crisis in whatsoever way seems to him best.

At last the hurly-burly's done; and the boss can look forward again to long months of peaceful possession. Most of those who have ventured to oppose him will soon seek his favor. Breaches of any consequence will quickly be healed; and the united strength of a dominant party will again, as always before, make the final election to office mere dumb show.

This unconscionable affair—which occurs at a point within fifteen minutes' walk of the Public Library and Trinity Church—is thus at once the climax and the résumé of local politics. It is calculated to arouse sombre reflections; for under the American system, the primary election is the nestling-place of our liberties.

[54.] *"A Spectacle . . . No Foreign Fiesta Could Equal"*

A newspaper correspondent describes a Republican "mass meeting" in a small Indiana town during the political campaign of 1876. [E. V. S., "Indiana Mass Meetings," *The New York Tribune*, September 23, 1876, p. 3.]

The scene is Cambridge City, a small place with a big name, containing perhaps 2,500 inhabitants . . . ; and the occasion is a speech by Gen. [Benjamin] Harrison, the Republican nominee for Governor. We arrive about noon with the orator of the day. At the railway station a company of men in Continental cocked hats and black oilcloth capes, trimmed with white, headed by a brass band, waits in line to receive him. While the band plays, the local committeemen put us in a barouche drawn by four fine white horses, with tall plumes nodding on their heads, and we move off in quite a triumphal fashion, the black-caped fellows going to the front to clear the way. As soon as we enter the street leading up to the village, we pass another long line of men wearing blue capes, and red, white, and blue caps, and carrying torches ready for service in the night parade. They fall in behind in good military way. At the next cross street there is a squadron of mounted men in scarlet trousers and white shirts waiting on the right to swell the line, and on the left a large body of footmen in scarlet shirts and dark trousers, carrying polished tin lamps fixed above the visors of the red caps.

With much blowing of horns and beating of drums—for all these troops have bands of some sort—we at last gain the main street. It looks like an Italian town in carnival time, as far as the houses with their flags, festoons of evergreens, and Chinese lanterns are concerned, but in the roadway there is a spectacle which for gay colors, novel devices, and real picturesqueness, no foreign fiesta could equal—an American political procession. It is not yet complete or organized, for it is not to move until the speakers have had their dinner at the village inn, but the material is here. There are huge wagons built up with boards in pyramidal fashion to make seats for pretty girls dressed in white, and wearing coronets of gilt pasteboard. They represent, of course, the States of the Union. One of these great chariots has a canopy upon which stands the Goddess of Liberty, holding fast to a young tree that towers up to an astonishing hight, and flings out the Stars and Stripes from below its leafy crown. Another wagon contains two or three dozen gray-haired men who voted for Harrison in 1840 and are going to vote for his grandson in 1876. In another there is a glee club of young ladies and gentlemen singing campaign songs to the accompaniment of a cabinet organ and a key-bugle. A little white and blue cotton cloth for drapery, with evergreens, flowers, banners, and mottoes, gives a gala look to these processional wagons, which crowd the street as far as we can see. Quaintest of them all is one supporting a veritable log cabin. Smoke issues from the stick chimney and coon-skins are nailed upon the walls, while on the roof is a live coon, who appears to be trying to climb a sapling to get at a frightened and woful-looking Democratic rooster that is tied to a branch. As our barouche makes its way through the crowds, the people in the vehicles, on the sidewalks, and at the windows of the houses cheer their candidate vociferously, and he responds to their greetings with smiles and bows. The little town is full of music, dust, and noise.

A hasty dinner is eaten and we set out for the place of meeting, which of course is out-of-doors. The marshals dashing about on fine horses, with much display of gay-colored sashes, rosettes and saddle-cloths, get the procession in shape. As we leave the mile-long street at the top of a hill and turn into the fields we get a view of the line—a river of bright lines moving through the darker margin of lookers-on that line the way. What a striking spectacle it is! And what masses of people—men, women, and children! Where could they all have come from, for the village could not have contributed a hundredth part of them? They have come by rail from the towns, big and little, for twenty miles around, and in wagons, on horseback and on foot from all the neighboring country. Even more striking is the scene when the tide of humanity has spread itself over the great green field around the little beech grove where the seats and the platform are. The escort clubs in their many-colored uniforms move to and fro, or break ranks with volleys of cheers; the ponderous wagons unload their joyous freight; family parties in holiday attire picnic upon the grass; new delegations are constantly arriving with music and banners; there are troops of romping children, knots of rosy-cheeked girls walking with interlocked arms, young couples making love and eating luncheon at the same time; booths where rustics feast on lemonade and gingerbread. The earnestness of politics is tempered with much merry-making, and the air is vocal with laughter, cheers, and songs. What a scene for a painter! How characteristically American and how rich in elements of the picturesque!

Only a small part of the throng can get within range of the orator's voice, but the rest seem none the less happy, for it is the holiday diversion, the crowds, the bravery of the procession, the music, and the fun of the occasion they came chiefly to enjoy. As many people as can possibly hear pack in upon the seats rising amphitheater-like against a sloping hill, or make a thick fringe around their margin. It is an attentive audience, quick to applaud a good point, and relishing keenly a funny story or witty remark. Nearly half the listeners are ladies. The speaker, Gen. Harrison, is a man of medium hight, compactly built, with a frank countenance, bright blue eyes, light-brown hair, and blonde beard. In conversation his manner is quiet, rather reserved, entirely unassuming, yet self-possessed; but on the stump he takes hold of his audience as if it belonged to him, and keeps it easily in his control as long as he wishes. He talks for an hour and a half about the war and the record of the Democratic party, and even goes way back to the Fugitive Slave law in hunting out the bad points in the record. There is almost nothing in his speech, except a brief reference to the Presidential candidates, that might not have been said just as well four years ago, or eight years ago; but the people are pleased with it. Evidently in their minds the memories of the Rebellion have but to be roused to supplant all later issues. A speaker from New-York talks for a short time on civil service reform and Tilden's railroad operations and income tax, and then the meeting ends with a count of the 1840 voters in the crowd.

In the evening the citizens, such as are not Democrats, light up their houses and hang out Chinese lanterns, and the uniformed clubs parade the streets with torches. There is more speaking, this time from a rude platform at a street corner, and wherever one goes about the place there is a blaze of light and an uproar of drums and fifes and brass bands, of men vociferating campaign songs or hurrahing for Hayes and Wheeler, for Harrison, and for Tom Browne (the candidate for Congress) as if they were wound up and could not stop. It is nearly midnight before the last club gets away on the cars and the last string of vehicles departs for the country.

[55.] From Hymn-Singing Hayes to "Godlike" McKinley

Julia B. Foraker, a frequenter of the White House during these years, chats intimately about four leading Republicans. [Julia B. Foraker, *I Would Live It Again: Memories of a Vivid Life* (New York: Harper & Brothers Publishers [now Harper & Row, Publishers, Inc.], 1932), pp. 69-70, 74, 130-33, 258-60, 267. © 1932 by Julia B. Foraker, renewed 1960 by Florence M. Foraker Matthews. Reprinted by permission of the publisher.]

The 'seventies were not decorative years, but Opportunity strode through them. While Foraker competed with the three hundred lawyers, I rocked cradles, copied legal documents for my husband in an earnest, ladylike hand, struggled with the *Buckeye Cook Book* and other facers, yet in all was buoyed by the pleasantest of convictions, that of getting ahead. The period brought Foraker his first elective office, judge of the Cincinnati Superior Court, and me my first visit to Washington.

President Hayes was in the "Executive Mansion" then. It was President Roosevelt who restored the charming old name, the "White House." Through my father, who spent much of his life in Congress, I seemed to have known the Hayeses always. The striking thing about the domestic atmosphere they created was their temperance hospitality (ah, but didn't that take courage then!) and their Sunday-night hymn-singing.

Those Sunday nights were so often described to me that I knew every detail of the scene before I ever saw it: the heavy ebony furniture; the crimson satin curtains, fearfully and wonderfully draped; the potted plants scattered all about the room; the dripping candles; the hot fire, one huge lump of anthracite! and Lucy Webb Hayes, in hoop-skirted black velvet, illusion, and seed pearls, at a gloomy Chickering square piano playing hymns while the guests, a crowd of people, sang with heart and soul . . .

"A few more years shall roll"

or

"There *is* a land of *pure* delight
Where saints immortal stand"

or, even the grovelling "worm hymns" which preceded Moody and San-key.

My own Sunday night début at the Hayeses' was on an occasion that was almost worldly. General Sherman was there. He was a great star, very human, very lovable, and wildly idolized. Whenever he appeared there was a sort of riot to do him honor. And riot there was this night. No one had need of hymns with "Tecumseh" to worship; the Hayeses wisely didn't bring out the books.

•   •   •

There was something very fine about Mr. and Mrs. Hayes. They did unpopular things, as their wineless dinner-giving, but it was with such thoroughbred courtesy that no one could resent it. They stood quite simply by the principle which they had brought with them to the White House. The Presidency could not swerve them from what they believed to be right. I think, however, that total abstinence was more her creed than his; but he yielded to her on this issue as on others. It has been pointed out sufficiently that Rutherford B. Hayes was utterly lacking in the politician's sense of politics. Just did what his standards obliged him to do. Did that —and served three terms as Governor of Ohio! His disinterestedness disarmed the most ax-grinding ward heeler.

•   •   •

The Harrison administration, beginning in 1889, was marked by one of the strangest personalities that ever found a place in the sun. Benjamin Harrison was a Presbyterian with a firm, doctrinal belief, which he was heard to express, that he had been predestined to occupy the presidential chair. Unfortunately, predestination failed to provide for a second term; indeed, it hardly insured the predestinee temperament enough to get him through the first. If "anything in the shape of a human being" interested Abraham Lincoln, nothing much in the shape of one brought a gleam to the eye of our aristocratic twenty-third President.

This lack of human sympathy, personal magnetism, what you will, was emphasized by the excessive magnetic charm of the Secretary of State. Blaine was idolized as no other political leader ever was, within my knowledge. Rather an over-rival for any man—the "plumed knight." But the difference between the Secretary and his chief was of the heart, which made it quite hopeless.

I remember once during the governorship when we were on a flying visit to Washington, my husband came back to the hotel looking as if he had had a chill. It was thus: business matters that day had taken Foraker to the State Department to see Mr. Blaine. He found the Secretary obviously overwhelmed with affairs; crowds of men were waiting to see him. Foraker at that time was concerned about the grave condition of his father's health. The newspapers were reporting this anxiety. Blaine saw my husband at once; came out to greet him; instantly detached himself from the scene, from everybody.

"Tell me about your father," he said, drawing Foraker into a private room: "Do you know that I've always thought of him as a tall, spare man? I never thought of him as a man who would have a stroke."

Foraker was so touched that he could hardly speak. Blaine had never even seen his father, but he knew how Foraker loved him and he kept him a long time to hear about their life together.

Then the Secretary plunged into politics, discussing, with complete knowledge and understanding, the condition and the needs in all their variations of the eighty-eight counties of Ohio. Blaine, Secretary of State —his hands full of our virgin-new foreign relations—had the facts about each one of those eighty-eight Ohio counties at his finger ends; knew all about them, couldn't have known more if that state had been his chief, his only interest. The President, like his Secretary, was a demon of energy, and doubtless his intelligence was as fine as Blaine's; but it was Blaine who radiated glamour and warmth when he did things. Had he been a woman, people would have rushed off to send expensive flowers.

When the Secretary and the Governor's talk ended, Blaine insisted that Foraker must have his, Blaine's, carriage to take him wherever business called him further, waved aside protests, ordered it immediately. And then it was a warm good-by with a "Do you know I have a feeling, a very strong feeling, that your father is going to pull through," and a hand-clasp that showed that he meant what he said. I think the secret of Blaine's extraordinary charm was that he really did care.

Glowing and happy from his visit with the Secretary, Foraker went directly from the State Department to the White House to pay his respects to the President. Mr. Harrison was very much himself.

"I've got all these papers to look after," he said, glancing at his desk, "and I'm going fishing at two o'clock." He snapped his watch.

It was not that the President was unfriendly to Foraker—far from it. It was just his way of being nice to the Governor of Ohio. Decidedly I thought my husband had had a chill when I saw him shortly afterward. I wondered what I ought to do for him. This benumbing frigidity in Harrison was what made him so good a friend to Cleveland in 1892. I don't think there was a single Republican who had the slightest idea that Harrison would be re-elected. How could he be? He had a trick of turning a Republican into a Democrat that was almost sleight-of-hand.

Harrison spoke extraordinarily well; probably no presidential candidate ever spoke better. He was always clear, forceful, vigorous, and always fresh. My father, who was in the thick of the campaign and heard hundreds of the speeches, said that Harrison *never once* repeated himself. This was a remarkable record, perhaps an unequaled one. Harrison was the first to make popular the front-porch campaign which later McKinley carried on at Canton. Each delegation was received with a speech that directly appealed to the district it represented and which captivated by its sympathetic, intimate understanding of individual conditions and its mastery of facts. The fine Harrison homestead in Indianapolis was devastated by the crowds which flocked to hear the candidate speak; Republican fans even carried off the fence. Harrison in 1888 did as much by his front-porch eloquence to help his cause as McKinley did to help his in 1896. If people could have just heard those splendid speeches, just heard Harrison, and then gone straight home and remembered how fine it was and never, never tried to shake the speaker's hand that was so like a wilted petunia— well, history might have been different.

· · ·

We were often at the White House from the beginning of McKinley days there. A worldlier note had crept in since my first acquaintance with it in Hayes' time. Instead of the Hayes hymn-singing, highly-paid artists were intrusted to furnish the music. I remember Nordica singing "Home, Sweet Home" one night; it was at Mr. McKinley's rather diffident request, with a narrow glance at his wife for fear the song might make her sad. Apprehension checked the spontaneity for which we were so ready when, with the Roosevelts, it very brilliantly came.

· · ·

The homage lavished by her husband Mrs. McKinley repaid with an adoration that quite upset values, just as the indulgence she had received made her look upon herself as different from all other women. Indeed, one had to watch one's *p's* and *q's* in conversation! I remember the confusion of a young English girl, guest of the Hobarts, at a White House dinner party. In reply to some bantering question she had admitted that, even after seeing America, she still loved England best; for her it was the place above all others in which to live.

Mrs. McKinley looked at her severely: "Do you mean to say that you would prefer England to a country ruled over by *my husband*?" She waited for an answer. There was no answer but an English blush. It may have been at the same dinner, or at another, that my husband, sitting next to Mrs. McKinley and doing his best with the difficulties of small talk with his hostess, remarked: "Your husband is lucky. He doesn't have to go home to vote. Now I have to drop everything and go out to Ohio (spring election) to vote."

Mrs. McKinley: "Well, I'm glad to hear that. I think it's about time you men did something. My husband has carried the Republican Party for twenty years. Now I'd like to see somebody else do something."

When anyone referred to the President's resemblance to Daniel Webster or to Napoleon, Mrs. McKinley waved the compliment aside as one not so much honoring McKinley as the other man. Her husband was the Hero of all Time—why "drag in" anybody else? Whatever the President felt about such rebuttals, his face betrayed nothing.

•   •   •

I doubt if the death of any public man ever caused more genuine sorrow in the hearts of his followers. McKinley had an almost mesmeric quality that made those who came under its spell add to the fine traits he possessed others more or less godlike. At the moment when Fate touched him with martyrdom these worshipers sometimes parted with their sense of humor to an extent that would have made their loved-and-lost hero himself smile. There was Captain Clark Toner, an old army comrade whom the President had appointed to the Indian Office, or maybe the Land Office. . . .

"He was the *purest* man that ever lived," said Toner. "Often, often I've heard him say, 'Boys, if there's any dirty work to be done, don't tell me of it. *Do it*—but don't tell me!' "

Tears streamed down the veteran's furrowed cheeks.

CIVIL SERVICE REFORM

[56.] *"Unfitness Is . . . Perpetuated"*

Julius Bing, an aide to Congressman Thomas A. Jenckes, tells why the civil service needs reforming. [Julius Bing, "Civil Service of the United States," *The North American Review*, CV, No. 217 (October 1867), 478, 488-91.]

The condition of the civil service of the United States is deplorable. Even in the early days of the Republic, although great care was taken to select for office only men of respectable character and qualifications, the need of a system of competitive examination was felt. But no such system was established, and, as far as the holders of office were concerned, a change for the worse took place in proportion to their increasing numbers and the vast increase of public business consequent upon the rapid strides of our progress. Nothing was done to adapt the civil service to the exigencies of the new times. Everything, on the contrary, combined to encumber its natural complications with abnormal difficulties growing out of partisan animosities.

• • •

. . . There is hardly a civilized country without a system of examination and promotion in the dispensation of its public offices.

Ours is probably the only country in the world where it does not exist in the civil service, though it exists in our military and naval service, the stringent discipline and efficiency of which are well known to all Americans. No doubt, the so-called localization of offices and political influences have heretofore impeded reform, nor do we desire to disregard this influence. Illinois, for instance, or Wisconsin, would be justified in complaining if their citizens were studiously kept out of all public offices, so that they might be filled exclusively by citizens of Massachusetts or of New Hampshire. The proper theory of the matter is, that all States should have the same right to competition, and that rejection should not take place upon any other ground excepting that of disqualification. Mr. Jenckes strikes the key-note in basing his bill upon the principle of *admission open to all.*

Another argument against the reform of the present chaos is the fear of a permanent bureaucracy, and of the anti-republican tendencies of such permanent institutions. We entertain no such apprehensions. A permanent bureaucracy is only dangerous when it is *incompetent and practically irresponsible.* We have already shown to what a great degree our service is now practically irresponsible, and we will proceed to show that it is a permanent institution, that we actually now have a permanent bureaucracy.

In the absence of a qualification test, it matters very little whether the incumbents of public offices represent the outgoing or the ingoing administration. If Jones, appointed in 1857, is of the same calibre as Smith, nominated in 1861, and Brown, in 1865, the fact of permanency is not in the least impaired by Jones being superseded by Smith, and by Brown supplanting Smith. Jones, Smith, and Brown, though three different persons,

are, in point of fact, one and the same individuality as far as their un-
qualified office-holding and their unfitness are concerned. This, indeed,
is the worst of all permanent bureaucracies, when the hydra-headed brood
of office-holders has positively one head, as far as qualification is concerned, and that head a dead-head. Unfitness is consequently perpetuated
to such an extent that, although Jones is removed, and Smith dies, and
Brown resigns, and White is promoted, the permanency of stupidity is
more and more consolidated as time passes on and generation succeeds
generation. The spectre "Red Tape," which we all imagined to have been
buried amidst the rubbish of antediluvian monarchies, is thus actually
haunting the public offices of the Republic. The American citizen, buoyant
with capacity, impatient of pedantry, finds himself, on crossing the thresh-
old of government offices, suddenly transferred from the nineteenth century of steam and telegraphs, to "the good old times of King George the
Fourth." Red-tape Jones of 1857 left a tradition of routine behind him,
which is cherished by red-tape Brown of 1861, which is still more enthusi-
astically adored by red-tape Smith of 1865, and which becomes the official
gospel of red-tape White of 1867.

• • •

Mr. Jenckes's bill . . . deserves the warmest support, as much for the
improvements which it actually proposes to enact by the introduction of
open competitive examinations in the subordinate branches of the home
civil service, and by the abolition of the system of irresponsibility and
patronage, as for the way in which it prepares for the adoption of reforms
in the foreign service and in all other administrative branches of the government.

The United States have gone through a formidable convulsion, the
outbreak of which was fomented to a great extent by wrong men in wrong
places; by faithless and reckless public officers at home and abroad; by
a demoralization of the public service, which was at the same time the
cause and the effect of treasonable practices and debasement of appointments to public offices to the vilest uses. The moral atmosphere of the
land is now gradually clearing up. The destructive era is drawing to
a close, and the constructive era is beginning to dawn. We have purged
our civilization from the degrading system of slavery. We are now im-
pelled, by all the considerations which are sacred to the lover of his country's fame, to complete this task by reforming those evils in the public
service of the country that grew up to a great extent under the fatal influence of sham-Democratic and Slave-State supremacy.

[57.] *"One Real Fly in the Washington Amber"*

A Senator's wife discusses office-seekers. [Julia B. Foraker, *I Would Live It Again: Memories of a Vivid Life* (New York: Harper & Brothers Publishers [now Harper & Row, Publishers, Inc.], 1932), pp. 215-17. © 1932 by Julia B. Foraker, renewed 1960 by Florence M. Foraker Matthews. Reprinted by permission of the publisher.]

There is, I consider, but one real fly in the Washington amber. One is penetrated at first by the charm of everything. How fluid and colorful the life is! So much movement! Such delightful people from all over the world! And then, presto! as by a swarm of locusts the land is darkened. The office-seekers have come to town! Every four years this phenomenon turns our exquisite national capital into a merry-go-round with a hoarse-voiced, brand-new crowd clamoring for place. The first two weeks after Foraker took his seat in the Senate he received more than twenty-five hundred letters from men who wanted a political office. This number was augmented, of course, by crowds of others at the official gates.

• • •

An office-seeker is a man who can't do anything but hold office. And he never really quite gives up. I used to receive a great many begging letters, myself. One I remember was from a woman who wrote me that her husband had voted for my husband at every election; he had just died. Now would I send her "a widow's mourning outfit, complete and up-to-date, and send so that *I'll get same by Wednesday,* madam." The italics are hers. So you see, even after an office-seeker dies his widow carries on.

[58.] *"The Fate of the Party . . .*
Lies in the Crossroads Post Offices"

A Democratic congressman defends the spoils system. [Frank
G. Carpenter, *Carp's Washington,* ed. Frances Carpenter
(New York: McGraw-Hill Book Company, 1960), pp. 120-22.
© 1960 by Frances Carpenter Huntington. Reprinted by permission of the publisher.]

A prominent Democratic Congressman talked freely to me last night
and defended the spoils system at length. He denounced Cleveland's
policy of not replacing Republicans in office with Democrats as detrimental
to the country and ruinous to the Democratic party.

"The fate of the party and the Administration lies in the crossroads post
offices," he said. "It makes little difference to the country at large what
they do with the jobs here in Washington, or those of our diplomats serv-
ing abroad. But if the postmasters are not changed, it is as though there
were no change in administration.

"When you think of the close relationships in a small town you can
see how such a principle acts. Take, for instance, the town of Pinhook in
my district. It has about three hundred people, a couple of stores, a blacksmith shop, and a post office. Its population is about equally divided between Democrats and Republicans, and it is always a question which way
it will go in an election.

"Smith, the present postmaster, is the leader of the Republicans, and
he works well for the party. He has his little row of post office boxes at
one end of his store counter. Everyone comes in to get his mail, and they
buy from him rather than from the other store, which is run by Democrat
Jones. When Smith puts up a pound of sugar, the paper he uses is a tract
on the tariff. If he sells a cake of soap, tales of Republican greatness are
printed on the paper in which he wraps that purchase. He sees that the
Republican county newspaper gets all the new subscribers, and when
subscriptions to the Democratic organ run out, he does not hurry to notify
the editor. Oh, he is useful to the party, all right.

"Across the road in the other small grocery and general store is Jones,
as ardent a Democrat as Smith is a Republican. He has worked for the
party through every campaign since 1860. At every election he has sent me,

as head of the Central Committee, twenty-five dollars for campaign expenses, has kept me posted on how the sentiment of the town is shaping up, and what we can do to be sure it votes Democratic. For years, however, the Republicans have won, and Smith, who is not a bad friend of his, has crowed over his success.

"Now at last the Democrats are in, so Jones decides to go to Washington and see about getting the postmastership as his just due.

" 'Is there anything the matter with Postmaster Smith?' the Postmaster General asks. He has in mind the orders from the President that the fact that a man is a Republican is not enough cause for his removal.

" 'Why,' Jones replies, 'Smith's a Republican. He's the rankest, radicalest Republican in Wayback County, and he's been working against our party for years. I'm the Democrat. Of course there's nothing wrong with Smith; he's good and honest. But the people of Pinhook think he's been in office long enough. They want a Democrat.'

" 'Well, now, if Smith had stolen a mule, or if he didn't do his job of sorting the mail properly, then I could help you. But just that he is a Republican doesn't count now.'

"So Jones goes home in disgust, and every time he gets his mail in Smith's store, he curses the Administration under his breath. The Democratic voters of Pinhook do not know what to make of it. The Administration has not changed for them, and when the next campaign comes around they have no leader, and no contribution comes to headquarters from the disgruntled Jones."

My friend the Congressman grew more and more vehement.

"The civil service idea is the most ridiculous thing ever attempted in the domain of politics," he fumed. "If it governs the choice of the country postmasters, it should be equally good for higher offices. Take George Pendleton, the advocate—some say the engineer—of this damnable civil service plan! He spent three months in Washington after the election, and the result is that he turned a good man out of his job as Minister to Germany and got himself appointed there.

"Or even take the President. On this theory, Cleveland should have said to Arthur on March 4th, 'Mr. Arthur, it's true the people have chosen me to fill your place. But I believe that when a man is in office and is doing well, he should not be disturbed. Everyone says you are a good President, so I'll just go back to my law practice in Buffalo and leave you in the White House.' "

THE TARIFF

[59.] *"To Aggrandize Themselves at the Expense of Others"*

The nation's leading exponent of *laissez faire,* William Graham Sumner, lashes out against protection. [William Graham Sumner, "What is Free Trade?" *Good Cheer* (April 1886), reprinted in William Graham Sumner, *The Forgotten Man and Other Essays,* ed. Albert Galloway Keller (New Haven: Yale University Press, 1918), pp. 123-27. Reprinted by permission of Yale University Press.]

Our intercourse with foreign nations . . . has been interfered with, because it is a fact that, by such interference, some of us can win advantages over others. The power of Congress to levy taxes is employed to lay duties on imports, not in order to secure a revenue from imports, but to prevent imports—in which case, of course, no revenue will be obtained. The effect which is aimed at, and which is attained by this device, is that the American consumer, when he wants to satisfy his needs, has to go to an American producer of the thing he wants, and has to give to him a price for the product which is greater than that which some foreigner would have charged. . . . Under this system a part of our product is diverted from the satisfaction of our needs, and is spent to hire some of our fellow-citizens to go out of an employment which would pay under the world's competition, into one which will not pay under the world's competition. We, therefore, do with less clothes, furniture, tools, crockery, glassware, bed and table linen, books, etc., and the satisfaction we have for this sacrifice is knowing that some of our neighbors are carrying on business which according to their statement does not pay, and that we are paying their losses and hiring them to keep on.

Free trade is a revolt against this device. It is not a revolt against import duties or indirect taxes as a means of raising revenue. It has nothing to say about that, one way or the other. It begins to protest and agitate just as soon as any tax begins to act protectively, and it denounces any tax which one citizen levies on another. The protectionists have a long string of notions and doctrines which they put forward to try to prove that their device is not a contrivance by which they can make their fellow-citizens contribute to their support, but is a device for increasing the national wealth and power. These allegations must be examined by economists, or other persons who are properly trained to test their correctness, in fact and logic. It is enough here to say, over a responsible signature, that no such allegation has ever been made which would bear examination. On the contrary, all such assertions have the character of apologies or special pleas to divert attention from the one plain fact that the advocates of a protective tariff have a direct pecuniary interest in it, and that they have secured it, and now maintain it, for that reason and no other. The rest is all afterthought and excuse. . . .

The protectionists, in advocating their system, always spend a great deal of effort and eloquence on appeals to patriotism, and to international jealousies. These are all entirely aside from the point. The protective system is a domestic system, for domestic purposes, and it is sought by domestic means. The one who pays, and the one who gets, are both Americans. The victim and the beneficiary are amongst ourselves. It is just as unpatriotic to oppress one American as it is patriotic to favor another. If we make one American pay taxes to another American, it will neither vex nor please any foreign nation.

The protectionists speak of trade with the contempt of feudal nobles, but on examination it appears that they have something to sell, and that they mean to denounce trade with their rivals. They denounce cheapness, and it appears that they do so because they want to sell dear. When they buy, they buy as cheaply as they can. They say that they want to raise wages, but they never pay anything but the lowest market rate. They denounce selfishness, while pursuing a scheme for their own selfish aggrandizement, and they bewail the dominion of self-interest over men who want to enjoy their own earnings, and object to surrendering the same to them. They attribute to government, or to "the state," the power and right to decide what industrial enterprises each of us shall subscribe to support.

Free trade means antagonism to this whole policy and theory at every point. The free trader regards it as all false, meretricious, and delusive. He considers it an invasion of private rights. In the best case, if all that the protectionist claims were true, he would be taking it upon himself to decide how his neighbor should spend his earnings, and—more than that—that his neighbor shall spend his earnings for the advantage of the men who make the decision. This is plainly immoral and corrupting; nothing could be more so. The free trader also denies that the government either can, or ought to regulate the way in which a man shall employ his earnings. He sees that the government is nothing but a clique of the parties in interest. It is a few men who have control of the civic organization. If they were called upon to regulate business, they would need a wisdom which they have not. They do not do this. They only turn the "channels" to the advantage of themselves and their friends. This corrupts the institutions of government and continues under our system all the old abuses by which the men who could get control of the governmental machinery have used it to aggrandize themselves at the expense of others. . . .

The free trader further holds that protection is all a mistake and delusion to those who think that they win by it, in that it lessens their self-reliance and energy and exposes their business to vicissitudes which, not being incident to a natural order of things, cannot be foreseen and guarded against by business skill; also that it throws the business into a condition in which it is exposed to a series of heats and chills, and finally, unless a new stimulus is applied, reduced to a state of dull decay. They therefore hold that even the protected would be far better off without it.

[60.] *"To Discriminate in Favor of Our Own"*

William McKinley gives the classic protectionist view. [William McKinley, "The Value of Protection," *The North American Review,* CL, No. 403 (June 1890), 741-44.]

If revenue is the sole consideration, then the surest and most direct way is to put the duty upon those articles of foreign manufacture and production which, with a small and inconsiderable tax, will produce the largest volume of revenue; meaning, of course, those articles that we either do not produce at all or in such small measure as to fall greatly short of our domestic wants. . . .

Is it not better . . . that the income of the government shall be secured by putting a tax or a duty upon foreign products, and at the same time carefully providing that such duties shall be on products of foreign growth and manufacture which compete with like products of home growth and manufacture, so that, while we are raising all the revenues needed by the government, we shall do it with a discriminating regard for our own people, their products, and their employments? . . .

•   •   •

Now, whatever system will bring the largest liberty to the masses of our countrymen, the largest independence to the workman, the highest incentive to manual and intellectual effort, the better comforts and the more refining environments to the family, cannot be dear at any price. It must be conceded that the protective system has accomplished much in this direction; certainly more than any other system. It has dignified and elevated labor; it has made all things possible to the man who works industriously and cares for what he earns; it has opened to him every gateway to opportunity. We observe its triumphs on every hand: we see the mechanic become the manufacturer, the workman the proprietor, the employee the employer. It does not stifle, but it encourages, manly effort and endeavor. Is this not worth something? Is it not worth everything? Especially in a country like ours, where the government is founded upon the consent of the governed, where citizenship is equal, and suffrage without limit, is it not our plain duty to educate, improve, and elevate our citizenship, which is indispensable to the peace and good order of our communities, and the permanence of our institutions? And the system which secures these advantages in a larger degree than any other, as experience has demonstrated, is the protective system.

The Democratic free-trade Tariff-Reformers cry out against this system as narrow and restrictive. The formation of government anywhere is narrow and restrictive: otherwise there would be no occasion for separate governments. But the system in itself is neither narrow nor restrictive. It is free—freer than the fiscal system of any other government as applied to its own people. It is unrestrained throughout forty States and all the territories; it extends from ocean to ocean. No other nation has such freedom of international exchange as ours. No other people have so few restraints placed upon their commerce, their trade, and their labor. The Free-Trader wants the world to enjoy with our own citizens equal benefits of trade in the United States. The Republican Protectionist would give the first chances to our people, and would so levy duties upon the products of other nations as to discriminate in favor of our own. The Democratic party would make no distinction; it would serve the alien and the stranger: the Republican party would serve the State and our own fellow-citizens.

CURRENCY

[61.] *"They Are Political Vagabonds, Slanderers and Demagogues"*

Newspaperman Frank B. Tracy is contemptuous of the leaders of the Populist party, but finds the rank and file honest, intelligent—though misguided—men. [Frank B. Tracy, "Rise and Doom of the Populist Party," *The Forum,* XVI, No. 2 (October 1893), 240-41, 244-48.]

That party, in the first year of its national existence, made a record unparalleled in our history, well calculated to cause apprehension among the greater parties. It cast more than a million votes, or nearly as many votes as elected Abraham Lincoln; gave its Presidential candidate twenty-two electoral votes; carried four States and placed eight members in the House; and it has now five members in the Senate. The first definite, immediate steps toward the party's formation were taken about eight years ago, when Farmers' Alliances were organized in all the States of the West. These Alliances were at first purely local and industrial. The members held meetings to discuss crop conditions and the best methods in agriculture and horticulture. The three or four years following were disastrous to the farmers. Their crops failed, they were in want, and had little money, and their produce brought low prices. Distress and discontent came and clamors for assistance arose. Their minds, crammed with unformed socialistic ideas, were inflamed by Alliance orators and by the circulation of books of the Donnelly-Bellamy type. These Alliances determined, independently of one another, that monopolies were grasping the earth, that gigantic conspiracies were forming to enslave them, and that the moneyed classes were united against the masses. The fact that these conclusions were reached simultaneously and independently all over the West does not prove, as the Populists insist, that they are correct; but it does prove that the leaven administered by paternal legislation, after the close of the Civil War, was working throughout all the great social organism of the West. Yet these great uprisings and apprehensions indicated also real and serious grievances and burdens of injustice which bore heavily upon Western farmers. The three main grievances related to transportation, land and money.

• • •

. . . The party demands Government ownership of all land not held by actual settlers, Government ownership of all transportation facilities, and Government issue of all money by its fiat alone. The platform declaration on the subject of land is vague, and is a remarkable modification of the communistic ideas first preached by the leaders. With this plank few would quarrel, although the proposed reclamation of lands granted to the railways would be absurd, as nearly all the valuable land has been sold. The Government ownership of railways and other means of transportation is another of their tenets which is undergoing modification. It is still, however, a favorite hobby with thousands and is clearly a scheme of pure socialism. They do not seem to realize that the placing of the seven hundred thousand men now engaged with American railways alone in the hands of any political party, would make that party's dislodgment from power almost impossible and would ultimately lead to a despotism. Nor do they propose a way to secure the ten billion dollars necessary to acquire these railways, except possibly by peculiar and characteristic financial schemes. Indeed, it is marvellous how these men, no matter how ignorant and unlearned, will furnish readily and confidently solutions for all problems of finance—the most intricate, delicate and least understood of all Government concerns.

The chief underlying principle of all Populist financial schemes is fiat money. Free silver, a sub-treasury, *etc.,* are purely incidental. It is the cardinal faith of Populism, without which no man can be saved, that money can be created by the Government, in any desired quantity, out of any substance, with no basis but itself; and that such money will be good and legal tender, the Government stamp, only, being required. Free silver will bring some relief, but nothing permanent so long as "contraction of the currency" is possible. We must increase the volume of our currency; that is the desideratum. The Government, say the Populists, which by Protection rolls wealth into the manufacturer's lap, which constructs great harbors, buildings and defences, which gave us free land, pensions, bounties, railways, and created greenbacks, can do anything to increase our money supply. Nothing can give a clearer idea of the Populist view of money than this illustration given to me lately by one of the ablest Populists in the West: "The money-market is like the pork-market in which John Cudahy lost his millions. Eastern financiers and gold-bugs are attempting to corner the money-market, just as Mr. Cudahy attempted to corner the pork-market. Mr. Cudahy failed because the supply of pork was beyond his estimation. Wall Street is succeeding because the supply of money is limited. We insist that the Government should increase the circulating medium to $50 *per capita* and keep it there. As fast as the plutocrats gather in the money, the Government should issue more money until the money-corner is broken." Assuming that this absurd and ludicrous comparison is correct, one cannot help inquiring where the value of money would go after such a corner were broken. It is quite evident that it would go where Mr. Cudahy's pork went.

. . . The Populist faith in the "Gover'ment" is supreme. The Government is all-powerful and it ought to be all-willing. When a Populist debtor is approached by a creditor, his reply is actually often in these words: "I can't pay the debt until the Government gives me relief." This intervention or saving grace of the Government is a personal influence to him, a thing of life. What shall minister to a mind diseased like the Populist's? Only constitutional remedies.

The constituent elements of this party give significant hints as to its character. The rank and file are composed of honest, intelligent men, mild in language and demeanor. During the Omaha convention the writer met frequently and conversed with an old friend, a delegate from an Iowa county. He was a "logical" Populist. One could read and analyze the entire movement in that man's record, which has always been socialistic. When I first knew him he was a Granger, then he became successively a Greenbacker, a Prohibitionist and a Populist. He is a man in more than comfortable circumstances, intelligent, honest and a Christian. It was during his early struggle for subsistence that he became inoculated with the socialist virus, and it remains with him. On the day the convention assembled he exclaimed with fervor, "This campaign is opening just like the first Lincoln campaign." Although the adjectives, "honest," "sincere," and "earnest," may be applied to the followers, their antonyms fit the leaders. At least ninety per cent of these candidates and exhorters are destitute of personal or political integrity. They are political vagabonds, slanderers and demagogues. Their records in their former homes are unsavory. All of them keep in the sore spots of their minds the sad memories of conventions in which they were old party candidates to whom came overwhelming disaster.

•   •   •

It would be unfair to close this article without recounting the excellent results of the organization of this party in the Western States. Like all third parties, it has done the good work of breaking up old political rings and corrupt administrations, making a cleansing of the old parties imperative. . . . This is especially true in Nebraska, where the party passed the Australian ballot law and the maximum freight-rate law, an act reducing the extortionate freight-rates. . . . Other meritorious and just laws were passed by this legislature, directed by Populists. In spite of all the great pressure of the corporations, the Populists, by the aid of the Democrats, elected to the Senate an honest man, William Vincent Allen, against the chosen friend of the monopolists, the Republican candidate, the general solicitor of the Union Pacific railway. That election cost Mr. Allen just $74.25. This was probably the smallest sum by which a seat in the present United States Senate was secured. Mr. Allen is a Populist, with a head filled with wrong financial notions; but he is a conservative, pure, incorruptible man, who won renown as an eminent attorney and a just, upright judge, whose acts of kindness and charity are legion.

But the greatest benefit derived from this party's birth has been educational. The whole country has been filled with the desire and spirit of investigation, and questions respecting finance and Governmental functions have been studied by men and women as they are studied nowhere else in the world. Out of this Populist movement are gradually evolving sound arguments to counteract their fallacies, and in this fact lies the very means for accomplishing the party's overthrow.

[62.] *"You Shall Not Crucify Mankind Upon a Cross of Gold"*

William Jennings Bryan closes debate on the adoption of the 1896 Democratic platform and earns himself the nomination. [William Jennings Bryan, *The First Battle: A Story of the Campaign of 1896* (Chicago: W. B. Conkey Company, 1896), pp. 204-6.]

And now, my friends, let me come to the paramount issue. If they ask us why it is that we say more on the money question than we say upon the tariff question, I reply that, if protection has slain its thousands, the gold standard has slain its tens of thousands. If they ask us why we do not embody in our platform all the things that we believe in, we reply that when we have restored the money of the Constitution all other necessary reforms will be possible; but that until this is done there is no other reform that can be accomplished.

•   •   •

Mr. Carlisle said in 1878 that this was a struggle between "the idle hold-ers of idle capital" and "the struggling masses, who produce the wealth and pay the taxes of the country;" and, my friends, the question we are to decide is: Upon which side will the Democratic party fight; upon the side of "the idle holders of idle capital" or upon the side of "the struggling masses?" That is the question which the party must answer first, and then it must be answered by each individual hereafter. The sympathies of the Democratic party, as shown by the platform, are on the side of the strug-gling masses who have ever been the foundation of the Democratic party. There are two ideas of government. There are those who believe that, if you will only legislate to make the well-to-do prosperous, their prosperity will leak through on those below. The Democratic idea, however, has been that if you legislate to make the masses prosperous, their prosperity will find its way up through every class which rests upon them.

You come to us and tell us that the great cities are in favor of the gold standard; we reply that the great cities rest upon our broad and fertile prairies. Burn down your cities and leave our farms, and your cities will spring up again as if by magic; but destroy our farms and the grass will grow in the streets of every city in the country.

My friends, we declare that this nation is able to legislate for its own people on every question, without waiting for the aid or consent of any other nation on earth; and upon that issue we expect to carry every State in the Union. I shall not slander the inhabitants of the fair State of Massa-chusetts nor the inhabitants of the State of New York by saying that, when they are confronted with the proposition, they will declare that this na-tion is not able to attend to its own business. It is the issue of 1776 over again. Our ancestors, when but three millions in number, had the courage to declare their political independence of every other nation; shall we, their descendants, when we have grown to seventy millions, declare that we are less independent than our forefathers? No, my friends, that will never be the verdict of our people. Therefore, we care not upon what lines the battle is fought. If they say bimetalism is good, but that we cannot have it until other nations help us, we reply that, instead of having a gold standard because England has, we will restore bimetalism, and then let England have bimetalism because the United States has it. If they dare to come out in the open field and defend the gold standard as a good thing, we will fight them to the uttermost. Having behind us the producing masses of this nation and the world, supported by the commercial inter-ests, the laboring interests, and the toilers everywhere, we will answer their demand for a gold standard by saying to them: You shall not press down upon the brow of labor this crown of thorns, you shall not crucify mankind upon a cross of gold.

IMPERIALISM

[63.] *"A Feeling of Robust Americanism"*

Theodore Roosevelt regrets that "education seems to have destroyed the strong, virile virtues" and insists that a nation must be willing "to pour out its blood . . . like water" for "honor and renown." [Theodore Roosevelt, *American Ideals* . . . (3rd ed.) (New York: G. P. Putnam's Sons, 1899), pp. 240-44, 251-52, 266, 269-70.]

It is a matter of serious concern to every college man, and, indeed, to every man who believes in the good effects of a liberal education, to see the false views which seem to obtain among so many of the leaders of educated thought, not only upon the Monroe Doctrine, but upon every question which involves the existence of a feeling of robust Americanism. Every educated man who puts himself out of touch with the current of American thought, and who on conspicuous occasions assumes an attitude hostile to the interest of America, is doing what he can to weaken the influence of educated men in American life. The crude, ill-conditioned jealousy of education, which is so often and so lamentably shown by large bodies of our people, is immensely stimulated by the action of those prominent educated men in whom education seems to have destroyed the strong, virile virtues and especially the spirit of Americanism.

• • •

There are many upright and honorable men who take the wrong side, that is, the anti-American side, of the Monroe Doctrine because they are too short-sighted or too unimaginative to realize the hurt to the nation that would be caused by the adoption of their views. There are other men who take the wrong view simply because they have not thought much of the matter, or are in unfortunate surroundings, by which they have been influenced to their own moral hurt. There are yet other men in whom the mainspring of the opposition to that branch of American policy known as the Monroe Doctrine is sheer timidity. This is sometimes the ordinary timidity of wealth. Sometimes, however, it is peculiarly developed among educated men whose education has tended to make them over-cultivated and over-sensitive to foreign opinion. They are generally men who undervalue the great fighting qualities, without which no nation can ever rise to the first rank.

The timidity of wealth is proverbial, and it was well illustrated by the attitude taken by too many people of means at the time of the Venezuela trouble. Many of them, including bankers, merchants, and railway magnates, criticized the action of the President and the Senate, on the ground that it had caused business disturbance. Such a position is essentially ignoble. When a question of national honor or of national right or wrong, is at stake, no question of financial interest should be considered for a moment. Those wealthy men who wish the abandonment of the Monroe Doctrine because its assertion may damage their business, bring discredit to themselves, and, so far as they are able, discredit to the nation of which they are a part.

It is an evil thing for any man of education to forget that education should intensify patriotism, and that patriotism must not only be shown by striving to do good to the country from within, but by readiness to uphold its interests and honor, at any cost, when menaced from without. Educated men owe to the community the serious performance of this duty. We need not concern ourselves with the *emigré* educated man, the American who deliberately takes up his permanent abode abroad, whether in London or Paris; he is usually a man of weak character, unfitted to do good work either abroad or at home, who does what he can for his country by relieving it of his presence. But the case is otherwise with the American who stays at home and tries to teach the youth of his country to disbelieve in the country's rights, as against other countries, and to regard it as the sign of an enlightened spirit to decry the assertion of those rights by force of arms. This man may be inefficient for good; but he is capable at times of doing harm, because he tends to make other people inefficient likewise. In our municipal politics there has long been evident a tendency to gather in one group the people who have no scruples, but who are very efficient, and in another group the amiable people who are not efficient at all. This is but one manifestation of the general and very unwholesome tendency among certain educated people to lose the power of doing efficient work as they acquire refinement. Of course in the long run a really good education will give not only refinement, but also an increase of power, and of capacity for efficient work. But the man who forgets that a real education must include the cultivation of the fighting virtues is sure to manifest this tendency to inefficiency.

It is exhibited on a national scale by the educated men who take the anti-American side of international questions. There are exceptions to the rule; but as a rule the healthy man, resolute to do the rough work of the world, and capable of feeling his veins tingle with pride over the great deeds of the men of his own nation, will naturally take the American side of such a question as the Monroe Doctrine. Similarly the anæmic man of refinement and cultivation, whose intellect has been educated at the expense of his character, and who shrinks from all these struggles through which alone the world moves on to greatness, is inclined to consider any expression of the Monroe Doctrine as truculent and ill advised.

* * *

. . . No triumph of peace is quite so great as the supreme triumphs of war. The courage of the soldier, the courage of the statesman who has to meet storms which can be quelled only by soldierly qualities—this stands higher than any quality called out merely in time of peace. It is by no means necessary that we should have war to develop soldierly attributes and soldierly qualities; but if the peace we enjoy is of such a kind that it causes their loss, then it is far too dearly purchased, no matter what may be its attendant benefits. It may be that some time in the dim future of the race the need for war will vanish; but that time is yet ages distant. As yet no nation can hold its place in the world, or can do any work really worth doing, unless it stands ready to guard its rights with an armed hand. . . .

* * *

. . . It is very important that we should, as a race, keep the virile fighting qualities and should be ready to use them at need; but it is not at all important to use them unless there is need. . . .

* * *

. . . Every man among us is more fit to meet the duties and responsibilities of citizenship because of the perils over which, in the past, the nation has triumphed; because of the blood and sweat and tears, the labor and the anguish, through which, in the days that have gone, our forefathers moved on to triumph. There are higher things in this life than the soft and easy enjoyment of material comfort. It is through strife, or the readiness for strife, that a nation must win greatness. We ask for a great navy, partly because we think that the possession of such a navy is the surest guaranty of peace, and partly because we feel that no national life is worth having if the nation is not willing, when the need shall arise, to stake everything on the supreme arbitrament of war, and to pour out its blood, its treasure, and its tears like water, rather than submit to the loss of honor and renown.

[64.] *"We Had Supposed Ourselves*
. . . A Better Nation"

William James discusses the psychology involved in the declaration of war with Spain. [William James to François Pil-
lon, Cambridge, June 15, 1898, in *The Letters of William
James,* edited by his son Henry James (Boston: The Atlantic
Monthly Press, 1920), II, 73-74. © 1920 by Henry James, renewed 1948 by William James and Margaret James Porter.
Reprinted by permission of Paul R. Reynolds, Inc.]

How much has happened since I last heard from you! To say nothing
of the Zola trial, we now have the Cuban War! A curious episode of
history, showing how a nation's ideals can be changed in the twinkling of
an eye, by a succession of outward events partly accidental. It is quite
possible that, without the explosion of the Maine, we should still be at
peace, though, since the *basis* of the whole American attitude is the
persuasion on the part of the people that the cruelty and misrule of
Spain in Cuba call for her expulsion (so that in that sense our war is
just what a war of "the powers" against Turkey for the Armenian
atrocities would have been), it is hardly possible that peace could have
been maintained indefinitely longer, unless Spain had gone out—a con-
summation hardly to be expected by peaceful means. The actual declaration of war by Congress, however, was a case of *psychologie des foules,*
a genuine hysteric stampede at the last moment, which shows how unfortunate that provision of our written constitution is which takes the
power of declaring war from the Executive and places it in Congress.
Our Executive has behaved very well. The European nations of the
Continent cannot believe that our pretense of humanity, and our disclaim-
ing of all ideas of conquest, is sincere. It has been *absolutely* sincere!
The self-conscious feeling of our people has been entirely based in a
sense of philanthropic duty, without which not a step would have been
taken. And when, in its ultimatum to Spain, Congress denied any project
of conquest in Cuba, it genuinely meant every word it said. But here comes
in the psychologic factor: once the excitement of action gets loose, the
taxes levied, the victories achieved, etc., the old human instincts will get
into play with all their old strength, and the ambition and sense of

mastery which our nation has will set up new demands. We shall never take Cuba; I imagine that to be very certain—unless indeed after years of unsuccessful police duty there, for that is what we have made ourselves responsible for. But Porto Rico, and even the Philippines, are not so sure. We had supposed ourselves (with all our crudity and barbarity in certain ways) a better nation morally than the rest, safe at home, and without the old savage ambition, destined to exert great international influence by throwing in our "moral weight," etc. Dreams! Human Nature is everywhere the same; and at the least temptation all the old military passions rise, and sweep everything before them. It will be interesting to see how it will end.

But enough of this!—It all shows by what short steps progress is made, and it confirms the "criticist" views of the philosophy of history. I am going to a great popular meeting in Boston today where a lot of my friends are to protest against the new "Imperialism."

[65.] *"This Spasm of Folly and Delusion . . . Will Surely Pass"*

Senator George F. Hoar clashes with his party over Imperialism. [*Congressional Record*, 55th Cong., 3d sess. (January 9, 1899), pp. 494, 501-2.]

. . . I have believed religiously, and from my soul, for half a century, in the great doctrines and principles of the Republican party. I stood in a humble capacity by its cradle. I do not mean, if I can help it, to follow its hearse. I am sure I render it a service; I am sure I help to protect and to prolong the life of that great organization, if I can say or can do anything to keep it from forsaking the great principles and doctrines in which alone it must live or bear no life. . . .

I am to speak for my country, for its whole past and for its whole future. I am to speak to a people whose fate is bound up in the preservation of our great doctrine of constitutional liberty. I am to speak for the dead soldier who gave his life for liberty that his death might set a seal upon his country's historic glory. I am to speak for the Republican party, all of whose great traditions are at stake, and all of whose great achievements are in peril.

•   •   •

I do not agree, Mr. President, that the lesson of our first hundred years is that the Declaration of Independence and the Constitution are a failure, and that America is to begin the twentieth century where Spain began the sixteenth.

The Monroe doctrine is gone. Every European nation, every European alliance, has the right to acquire dominion in this hemisphere when we acquire it in the other. The Senator's [Orville H. Platt's] doctrine put anywhere in practice will make of our beloved country a cheap-jack country, raking after the cart for the leavings of European tyranny.

· · ·

Our fathers dreaded a standing army; but the Senator's doctrine, put in practice anywhere, now or hereafter, renders necessary a standing army, to be reenforced by a powerful navy. Our fathers denounced the subjection of any people whose judges were appointed or whose salaries were paid by a foreign power; but the Senator's doctrine requires us to send to a foreign people judges, not of their own selection, appointed and paid by us. The Senator's doctrine, whenever it shall be put in practice, will entail upon us a national debt larger than any now existing on the face of the earth, larger than any ever known in history.

Our fathers dreaded the national taxgatherer; but the doctrine of the Senator from Connecticut, if it be adopted, is sure to make our national taxgatherer the most familiar visitant to every American home.

Our fathers respected above all the dignity of labor and rights of human nature. The one thing created by God a little lower than the angels was a man. And they meant to send abroad the American flag bearing upon its folds, invisible perhaps to the bodily eye, but visible to the spiritual discernment, the legend of the dignity of pure manhood. That legend, that charter, that fundamental truth, is written in the opening sentences of the great Declaration, and now the Senator from Connecticut would repeal them. He would repeal the great charter of our covenant. No longer, as the flag floats over distant seas, shall it bear on its folds to the downtrodden and oppressed among men the glad tidings that there is at least one spot where that beautiful dream is a living reality. The poor Malay, the poor African, the downtrodden workman of Europe, will exclaim, as he reads this new doctrine: "Good God! Is there not one place left on earth where in right of my manhood I can stand up and be a man?" Will you disregard every lesson of experience? No tropical colony was ever yet successfully administered without a system of contract labor strictly administered and enforced by the Government. I will not speak of the thirteenth amendment. In our parliamentary practice amendments fall with the original bill. This amendment will fall with the original Constitution.

Mr. President, this spasm of folly and delusion also, in my judgment, will surely pass by. Whether it pass by or no, I thank God I have done my duty, and that I have adhered to the great doctrines of righteousness and freedom, which I learned from my fathers, and in whose service my life has been spent.

[66.] *"Imperialism Is the* New Treason"

A literary man writes Congressman George W. Julian condemning "McKinley's cussedness." [S. W. Stevens to George W. Julian, Lexington, Massachusetts, February 2, 1899, Joshua R. Giddings and George W. Julian Correspondence, Library of Congress, Washington, D. C.]

Yes, my dear sir, I felt certain that *you* must be opposed to the mad folly, not to say crime, of Imperialism. A man possessing such clear discernment as your public career has given rare evidence of could not fail to see that Imperialism is the *new treason* which now confronts and threatens our beloved nation,—treason to the very spirit and genius of our republic; treason to those high ideals that have given us all the greatness and glory which we can rightly lay claim to among the nations of history. The Republican party has many crimes to answer for at the bar of historic judgment, but none that is quite so damnable as this which its chosen President is now seeking to commit. He would publish us to the world as a nation of deliberate liars and pharisaical hypocrites. That in this he should seek the sanction of religion does not surprise me; for has not religion most times been ready to sanction villainy when it appeared in her name and wore her colors? "Duty and destiny!" cries Imperialism; "The gospel and salvation to heathen lands!" cries religion,— and away they both go, tails over the dasher, a well-matched pair, bearing with them to destruction the ark of our nation containing the Constitution and the Declaration. We in Massachusetts who love the old ideals of our republic hang our heads with shame when we see only one of our senators at Washington contending for these ideals. Oh that *our Lodge* were in some vast wilderness, among the clouted savages he is so anxious to annex, rather than in the Senate as our misrepresentative! Hoar, whom

I have never had any use for until now, is standing up nobly against the treaty which treats for war rather than peace, and I only hope that he will "stick," as Sumner advised Stanton to. We Anti-Imperialists in Massachusetts have done what we could to stem the tide of McKinley's cussedness. . . .